MOUNTAIN BIKE
NOVA SCOTIA

GEOFF BROWN
KERMIT DEGOOYER

W0009083

NIMBUS
PUBLISHING

Nimbus Publishing Limited
PO Box 9301, Station A
Halifax, NS B3K 5N5
(902) 455-4286

Design: Kathy Kaulbach, Halifax
Cover photo: Lawrencetown Rail Trail by Bob Brooks, Halifax
Printed and bound in Canada

Canadian Cataloguing in Publication Data
Mountain Bike Nova Scotia
Brown, Geoff, 1969–
ISBN 1-55109-155-0
Includes bibliographical references.
1. Bicycle trails–Nova Scotia. 2. Bicycle touring–Nova Scotia.
3. Nova Scotia–Guidebooks. I. deGooyer, Kermit. II. Title.
GV1046.C32N69 1996   796.6′4′09716   C95-950317-X

DISCLAIMER
Mountain bicycling is an unpredictable activity that will expose the enthusiast to a variety of risks and hazards. While we have taken care to accurately describe potential hazards along all of the routes in this book, no guide can substitute for common sense. Ride in anticipation of danger and know your limits. To the best of our knowledge, the directions and dis-tances provided are correct. However, we offer no guarantees. Anyone who enters the woods for any purpose risks getting lost. Always tell someone where you are headed and when you expect to return. The authors accept no responsibility for loss or injury resulting from the use of this guidebook.

Acknowledgements

We are indebted to several people and organizations who helped us complete this book. We extend our sincere thanks to students, staff and faculty of the Environmental Planning Dept. at the Nova Scotia College of Art & Design for giving us work space and creating a friendly working atmosphere.

We also thank the following people and groups for their assistance. Their help ranged from identifying some of the trails in this book and coming along on rides to supplying research materials and telling us some of the stories that we've passed on: Jim St. Clair, Bob & Beth Brooks, Darrin Aucterlonie, Tony Case at Slickrock Cycle, Jenny Gray, Gomer, Chris Kata, Norma MacIntyre at PowerBar Canada, Sean McDonough, Katrina McLaughlin, Dave Botten, Cheryl Baker and the Tourism Industry Association of NS, Jonathan Murphy, Neddy MacDonald, Dr. Derek Davis, the Colchester Historical Society, Bill Kenneally, Kyte Gillis, Ira & Bette Anne Corkum, Leona & Kilburn Currie, Annick de Gooyer, John Chisholm & Debbie Wallace at the Cooperation Agreement, the DNR firetower guys, Walter Jackson at the DOT Right of Way & Claims Office, John Cotton & the Inverness County Recreation Dept., John Leduc & Brian Kinsmen at the DNR Parks & Recreation Division, the Dalhousie University Map Collection, Jim MacLean, Ian Sherman, Jeff Feigin, Jim Lotz, Aunt Libby & Uncle Fred, maintenance guru Colin Matthews, Robert Redden at the DNR Land Administration Office, Dave "Reddy" Redwood, Steve Rolston, Dan Frid, Sandra Widmer, Carol & Cindy in Bear River, Marilyn Smith, Michael Haynes, Melvin and Debbie Burton, Jessie McKenzie, Rob Buckland-Nicks, Henri & Phyllis Steeghs, Todd Wallace, Ike Whitehead & Bicycle Nova Scotia, Tom Wilson at Victoria County Recreation, Alex Wilson at the NS Museum, Kathy Kaulbach, Dorothy Blythe and Joanne Elliott at Nimbus, and everyone else who helped us out.

This project received financial assistance from the Canada-Nova Scotia Cooperation Agreement on Sustainable Economic Development.

Contents

----

18 Mountain Bike Tours in Nova Scotia

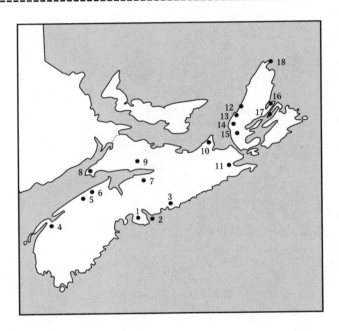

Leaving Fort McNab, McNabs Island.

Introduction

Welcome to "Canada's Ocean Playground"—mountain bike style! *Mountain Bike Nova Scotia* has been designed to help you explore the side of Nova Scotia that's off the beaten path. Follow the eighteen tours in this guide to discover rugged coastlines, mountains and glens, abandoned villages and forgotten farmsteads, old carriage routes, hardwood forests, giant tides, remote beaches, harbours, barrens, lakes and countless other attractions that haven't been watered down for general consumption.

Nova Scotia boasts a colourful cultural heritage and intriguing natural history that shouldn't be lost to mountain bikers. Along with the guides' detailed maps and directions, we've stuck in some tales and facts about each tour's hidden treasures, passed on from both written sources and local storytellers.

Designing a trail guide with universal appeal can be an overwhelming task when you consider that mountain biking has become as diverse as its participants. First are the racers, those weekend warriors who enjoy the exhilaration of pitting themselves against the competition. Next are the bikepackers, that select group of enthusiasts who preservere through multi-day wilderness treks, and the weekend cruisers, a relaxed crowd who dig an easy ride along a smooth bike path. Then there are cops and bicycle couriers who need their mountain bikes for work, and commuters who use them to get to work.

But amongst this diversity, it seems nearly everyone can get psyched for a day or afternoon ride in the country or backwoods. Again, some will prefer a challenging trip along a rugged trail while others will want to hang back on easier routes. This guide should offer something for everyone because the tours span a broad range of distances and difficulties. And they all take a day or less (we hope!) to complete. Those who are already exploring the province on their mountain bikes may notice that we have left out a few of the more popular trails. We regret that we couldn't include some great trails that run through private land. We also steered clear of designated and proposed wilderness areas, sensitive wildlife habitat and popular hiking trails. We hope cyclists finds the routes in this guide as exciting as we did and we wish you well on your adventures.

Using the guide and maps

The base maps used in this book contain geographic features, man-made structures, place names and contour lines. The contour lines show changes in elevation, usually at 15 m (50 ft.) intervals. Flat areas are shown by widely spaced contours, while contours that run close to one another indicate steep hills. The contours allow you to visualize the map in three dimensions and help with what orienteering types refer to as terrain association. Practice terrain association by finding significant landscape features (such as cliffs, hills or lakes) visually and then locating them on the map.

Over the base maps you'll see a bold line to show the route, an "S" to mark the starting point and arrows to show the direction of travel. A dashed line depicts alternate routes or optional shortcuts and offshoots. You'll also find distance scales (which vary from map to map) and a north arrow. Although the maps identify a handful of attractions for each tour, we encourage you to add more. Personalize your maps by pencilling in any additional discoveries, new turn-offs, scary dogs, etc.!

The maps and a bicycle computer *should* keep you from getting lost. Our trail descriptions include distances for landmarks along the trails. They also tell you where to turn and in which direction. Keep track of your progress by checking our distances with those on your bicycle computer. The two distances shouldn't be off by any more than 0.1 or 0.2 km (due to slight variations between different bicycle computers). If you don't have a computer, ride with someone who does, or consider buying one for yourself. It's not a must, but it will decrease your chances of getting lost and help you get more out of the trail descriptions. Your average bike computer sells for about $40.

Keep in mind that landmarks along trails will change over time. For example, what we describe as a left turn at the blue house with a red barn may someday become a left turn at the white house with half a red barn. Our advice, don't take the route descriptions *too* literally. When in doubt, explore. That's half the fun!

Safety
First Aid Kit

It's a good idea to bring along an emergency first aid kit every time you ride in a remote area. Pre-packaged kits are widely available at outdoor supply stores and are less expensive than assembling everything you need piece by piece. These kits also include things that you may not think to include yourself. Most come with a handy little instruction booklet. Know how to use each item in your kit before you hit the trail.

If you already have a kit, remember to restock it each time you use an item. Also, remember to check the condition of these items. Muddy water may have worked its way into your kit since the last ride and ruined some of the items. Try packing all of the items in zip-lock bags to avoid this.

Helmets

Wear one. To borrow from the Bell Helmets advertisement: "If you have a $10 head wear a $10 helmet." If your head's worth more than ten bucks get a helmet that's certified by either Snell or CSA. And make sure you wear it. A heavy and uncom-

Sandra "The Enforcer" Widmer making sure Dan is strapped in.

fortable helmet will probably end up on the back seat of your car while you're out on the trail. You can get your hands on a light, comfortable and well-ventilated helmet for around $50.

Hunting Season

Hunting season in Nova Scotia usually begins during the first week in October and ends on the first Saturday in December. Call your local Department of Natural Resources office to confirm the dates. If you venture out during hunting season, wear a hunter's orange vest regardless of whether or not you think there's any hunting going on in the area. Some people pull orange togues over their helmet. You might also consider staying home. Hunting is not permitted on Sundays.

Trail Hazards
Canine Encounters

Many of the trails featured in this guide go through rural areas where there's always a chance of encountering an over-zealous pooch. Always be on the lookout when passing any house that's near the trail. An aggressive dog poses a very real threat to your personal safety and you should do whatever it takes to protect yourself from a bite. Hopefully, you'll never experience a bite, but it's important to know what to do just in case. If a dog manages to sink his chops into you, rinse the wound with alcohol or peroxide and get medical attention immediately. Then, report the incident to the nearest police station or animal control office (in most rural areas this will mean a call to the local municipal building). We'll let you know where we encountered problems.

If you spot a dog before it spots you, silence is your best defence against a possible attack, especially if the animal is catching a lazy afternoon snooze. Stop talking, whistling or singing and above all keep pedaling. Pedal hard! Avoid coasting as your freewheel will begin clicking. If you can sneak by a dog without being noticed, you have avoided a potentially dangerous encounter.

In cases where the dog spots you first, don't stop. At about 25 clicks (15 mph), you can probably out-sprint most dogs on a flat stretch. If the pooch starts gaining on you though, don't take any chances. Get off your bike and use it as a barrier. Once you've stopped moving the dog may calm down and lose interest. A powerful squirt from your water bottle, right between the eyes, might also do the trick.

Bridges

Many of the trails described in this guide follow abandoned roads. Bridges on these old roads are often no longer maintained and many are rotten. Cross with caution. We often *walked* our bikes over or around scary looking bridges.

Fire Towers

Climb these at your own risk. The fire watchers we ran into usually enjoyed the company of a visitor, but they're not interested in coaxing anyone down the ladder. High winds and rain can make climbing surprisingly challenging.

Traffic

Beware of logging trucks and ATV's barrelling down dirt roads. They're not used to sharing the trail with bicycles.

Bugs

Mosquitoes and blackflies are the most obvious pests that you'll have to guard against while cycling in Nova Scotia. Beware of blackflies in the spring and mosquitoes in the summer. During these months consider packing some insect repellent. Have a look at the label before you purchase any bug dope. Many insect repellents contain DEET, a known carcinogen.

The western half of Nova Scotia becomes infested with the introduced American dog tick every spring. You should examine your arms and legs after the ride since you probably won't feel these sneaky insects crawling over your skin.

Climate

For those not familiar with Nova Scotia's weather we have two words: expect anything. If you are coming from away, the best time to visit Nova Scotia for mountain biking is during the summer and autumn months; spring tends to be a short, wet season.

Temperatures start warming up in April but the trails stay wet for quite some time. Snow cover doesn't completely disappear until the end of April (May in the highlands of Cape Breton). Thus, most trails begin to dry out around the first week of June.

Summer temperatures can reach 35°C (95°F) in July, especially inland, but they can also drop to around 10°C (50°F) along the coast. Rain is a possibility, regardless of the season; we recommend finding a spot in your pack for a light water-resistant shell.

Things start cooling down again around the end of September but you can ride comfortably well into November and December. For these months you'll need a pair of tights, an inner layer (preferably a polyester or cotton/polyester blend T-shirt), an insulating layer (light wool or fleece sweater), and a wind shell. A polyester or cotton/polyester blend T-shirt doesn't soak up as much water and dries out quicker than a regular cotton T-shirt. This will allow you to stay much warmer. Once cotton gets wet it stays wet, sucking valuable heat from your body. Full-fingered gloves are also a good idea in the fall.

Trail Mix
Water

Always carry more water than you expect to use. Two oversized water bottles per person should do for all of the trails featured in this guide. Drink small amounts of water throughout the ride, regardless of whether or not you feel thirsty. Thirst is a reaction to dehydration, something that you want to avoid. If you wait until you become thirsty you are already dehydrated.

Don't trust streams. The water may look clean (and often it is) but who knows what carcass is decomposing just upstream (animals sometimes go to streams to die) or where the nearest giardia-infected beavers are swimming.

Energy

It's a good idea to pack a PowerBar, some fruit or some trail mix on every ride. Go with something that you enjoy and that gives you a boost. PowerBars work well because they're packed with carbohydrates and replenish the body's energy stores as they're being used up. They also won't turn to mush when the going gets hot. You can get them at bike shops for about two bucks a piece.

Trail Ethics

While most of the trails featured in this guide are not promoted elsewhere for hiking or equestrian use, you may encounter both user groups during your travels.

Horses

Equestrian encounters can be quite an ordeal if you are unaware of the proper etiquette. Horses are plains animals and as such have large, widely spaced eyes that give them a wide visual field, which allows them to pick up movement over large distances; they are not good at picking up detail. As well, a horse has acute hearing but finds it difficult to pin-point the sources of sounds. As a result, a horse hears sounds before it knows where they are coming from. When you come around a blind curve and end up face to face (or face to rear!) with a horse, it senses a fast moving and foul smelling object. The horse doesn't know what you are or how close you are. Being in the wrong place at the wrong time can be dangerous for all parties involved.

Proceed with caution whenever you meet a horse and rider. When approaching from behind, signal your presence and keep well back until the rider knows you are there (words work better than bells). Ask the rider how best to proceed. Like people, horses have personalities and no one knows an individual horse's personality better that its rider. For a face to face encounter, stop all forward movement immediately (but without skidding). Make verbal contact with the rider and speak to the horse in a calm tone as you move slowly off the trail. If the trail cuts across a slope, always move off to the downhill side. When space is limited, retreat to an area where the horse can safely pass. Keep your distance in case old wildheart decides to deliver a parting kick. Don't expect the horse and rider to retreat. It's much easier for you to spin your bike 180° than it is for an equestrian to turn a horse around.

Hikers

Hikers are another user group that deserve our consideration. Mountain bikers negotiate trails much faster than hikers. In some cases hikers resent mountain bicyclists merely because they are startled by them. If you can avoid startling hikers by signaling your presence you've done a lot to improve trail relations. To quote mountain bike cartoonist and riding guru William Nealy, "Consider yourself the Supreme Ambassador of the Mountain Bike Nation." When riding in a group, let everyone behind you know that there are hikers up ahead. Say hello to make the hiker aware of your approach. Control your speed and approach turns in anticipation that someone or something may be just around the bend. Yield the trail whenever you meet a hiker on singletrack.

Treading lightly

For many mountain bikers, a large part of the riding experience involves getting away from the city to enjoy nature. So it's only fitting that we all make an effort to preserve the trails and wilderness that we're out to enjoy. Here are some general guidelines, adapted from the International Mountain Bicycling Association, that will reduce the stress on Mother Nature.

• Avoid riding after heavy rains. Water loosens soil and makes the ground susceptible to erosion. Riding a really wet trail tears it apart.

• Use one gear higher than normal when conditions are dry. This will reduce tire spinning and result in less damage to the trail.

• Keep your brakes properly adjusted. They shouldn't begin to engage until about halfway through the stroke of the brake lever. Properly adjusted brakes give you better braking control and minimize brake-induced skidding. Skidding can cause a lot of damage to trails by increasing the amount of loose soil available for erosion. Ride, don't slide.

- Keep your tire pressure at about 40 psi or lower. A lot of people fill their tires to 60 psi. to increase efficiency while riding on the road. The lower pressure not only does less damage to the trail but it's also easier on your body (by softening the ride).

- Pedal through puddles rather than walking or riding around them. By going around wet spots many cyclists contribute to trail widening and trample trail-side vegetation. In extreme cases, trail widening can be a problem both environmentally and aesthetically.

- Avoid blasting through streams. If there's no bridge, jump across on some stones or walk through. Stirring up sediment can harm fish and other critters that rely on clean, clear water.

- Never leave the trail and cut across vegetation, sand dunes or other sensitive areas.

- Pack out what you pack in.

Trail Fix
Assembling An Emergency Repair Kit

An emergency repair kit is an absolute requirement on any ride. Unlike road riding, where you can make it home with nothing more than some change for the phone, a quarter just doesn't cut it out in the woods. We suggest including the following items in your **emergency repair kit:**

- 6" adjustable wrench
- small Phillips screwdriver
- 1/8" flathead screwdriver
- 4, 5 and 6 mm allen keys (If your crankarms require an allen key bring one large enough for them)
- small folding knife
- patch kit
- 2 tire levers
- spoke wrench
- spare tube
- mini-pump
- tire boot
- chain tool
- cloth or nylon braided tape
- hockey or duct tape
- a couple of loonies

Most cycling shops sell tools that combine the features of several tools into one unit. They will save you space and weight. The most basic models combine three allen keys, a small knife, a Phillips screwdriver and a flathead screwdriver. Others combine tire levers, spoke wrenches and chain tools.

It's also a good idea to wrap all of your tools (except for the tube and mini-pump) in a piece of white cloth and hold it together with an elastic (preferably a nylon covered hair elastic, it's less likely to break). When you have to make repairs on the trail, the white cloth can act as a travelling work bench. Lay everything on the cloth and it'll be easier to keep track of small nuts and screws.

Remember to check the glue in your patch kit often. If it's been more than a year since you last patched a tube, the glue has probably turned to dust by now.

Quick Fixes
Stripped pedal
If your pedal falls out the crankarm threads could be stripped. Remedy the problem by threading the pedal in from the back of the crankarm. This re-taps the threads. Remove the pedal and try it from the proper side. This should at least get you home.

Warped rim
If your wheel is bent so badly that it can't spin freely, remove the wheel and bend it back into shape. Start by bracing the hub of the wheel against a large object such as a rock, tree or stump. Then apply as much force as is necessary. You may find it necessary to use your legs for this.

Bent handlebars
Remove the seat post and slide it on over the end of the bar that is bent (if you have bar ends you'll have to remove them). The seat post should provide you with enough leverage to bend the bar back into shape. Don't use enough force to bend your seat post as well. Remember, those bars are much weaker now than they were before, so go easy on them. Once they've been

bent, your bars are toast. Trash them for new one's before the next ride.

Broken spoke
Tape a broken spoke to its neighbour. If you pull it out, you'll have to find some place to put it so you might as well leave it attached.

Broken saddle
Your bicycle seat is one of the most vulnerable components in a crash. The most common problem is the seat coming unattached from its rails.

If this happens, place the seat back on its former position on the rails. Now take that handy roll of tape

Checkin' out the maps in the parking area at Jimmy's Roundtop.

that you packed and begin securing the seat to the rails by taping over and under the seat in a figure eight pattern. Again, you'll need to purchase a new seat once you get home but at least you won't have to stand for the remainder of the ride.

Avoiding a trail fix: a pre-ride check-list
• Carefully check all the spokes on both rims by squeezing them together in pairs. Any loose spokes should be tightened.
• Inspect the tires for cracks, cuts or wear (fuzzy sidewalls are a bad sign). Replace any tire that looks like it could blow out. All inner tubes gradually leak air over time so check the pressure and top off as needed.

- Test your brakes by giving the levers a squeeze. People often remove their wheel and forget to hook up the brakes. Also, check the brake pads for excessive wear and replace as necessary.
- Check the headset and bottom bracket. For the headset, lift the front end of the bike with one hand and grab the fork with the other. Now, try to rock the fork back and forth in the head tube. If you know how, tighten the headset (if not, go to a local bike shop and have someone do it for you). Next, with the front tire still off of the ground, gently turn the handlebars back and forth through the entire turning radius. The bar should turn smoothly. If it is notchy or locks into place, have the headset adjusted or repacked before the next ride.

To check the bottom bracket, grab both crank arms and try to rock them back and forth. There should be no movement. If there is, tighten the bottom bracket as soon as possible. The more you ride with a loose bottom bracket the worse it gets. Now, try spinning the crankarms (you'll have to remove the chain for this). They should spin smoothly and evenly. If they stop suddenly, the bottom bracket is adjusted too tightly and should be loosened or checked for debris.

Check at your local bike shop for books on mountain bike maintenance. Some Nova Scotia bicycle shops give hands-on mechanics courses as well. Slickrock Cycle in Dartmouth (902-434-6266) offers both a beginners and a Level II course. They also rent tool and work space.

HALIFAX COUNTY

Jimmy's Roundtop

Starting Point: Hubley, Halifax County. Take Exit 4 off
Highway 103 and head west 2.5 km on Route 3 to
Hubley. Turn left across the old railbed and then make
a quick right. Stay on the paved road until it dead ends
(about another 2.5 km past the old railroad crossing).
Do not continue straight onto the dirt road as it leads
into the Three Brooks subdivision.

Length:	29.2 km
Difficulty:	moderate, a few rolling hills and lots of bumps
Trail Type:	boulder-strewn dirt roads and wagon tracks
Riding Time:	half day at least

This is a rocky ride across the barrens of Jimmy's
Roundtop, down to St. Margarets Bay and then back
along the Woodens River. We'll ride sections of the Old St.
Margarets Bay Road and Old Halifax Road, both bumpy
trails that once connected Halifax with outports along the
bay. Built two hundred years ago, the Old Halifax Road

Rock hop dogin' over another rough section at Jimmy's.

was the first overland link between these isolated communities and Halifax. Before its construction, people relied on boats as the only means of transportation between the two areas. Even after roads were built, conditions were so poor that by 1815 boats remained the preferred way to travel. From all accounts, both the Old St. Margarets Bay Road and the upper section of the Old Halifax Road are probably in much the same condition now as they were then. When you get out onto the trail you'll realize how difficult it must have been to get a horse and buggy through there. Too bad they didn't have mountain bikes two hundred years ago!

0.0   Head down the wagon track and cross the small bridge over Flake Brook.

1.7   Continue STRAIGHT past the right offshoot.

2.0   Keep LEFT at the V in the trail. The smaller track on the right is where you'll finish the loop.

2.7   Make a hard LEFT as you continue past the right offshoot leading to Long Lake.

3.3   The trail takes a sharp RIGHT. You should see a large rounded hill off in the distance. That's Jimmy's Roundtop!

3.5   Pass a sign on the right that says "Rough Section Next 7.3 km," a pretty accurate description of the remainder of the ride.

3.6   Continue STRAIGHT past an offshoot on the left.

4.0   The right offshoot leads to Long Lake. Continue STRAIGHT.

4.7   As you head down into Woodpecker Hole you'll notice an abundance of red oak on the left side of the trail.

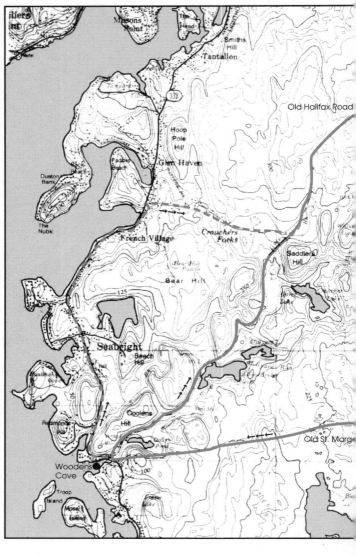

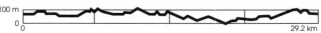

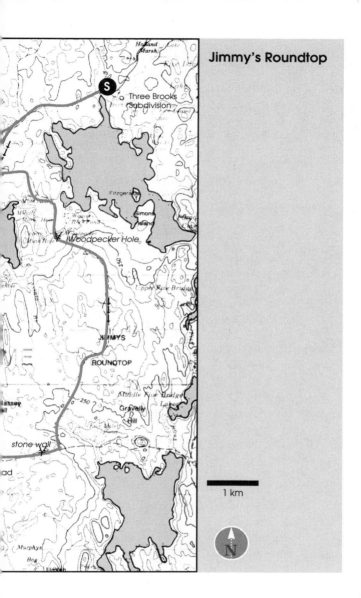

Jimmy's Roundtop

1 km

N

> **Red oak** are in decline in some parts of Nova Scotia but they flourish here along with aspen, white birch and red maple. All of these hardwoods do well in rocky soils that have been ravaged by fire. Forest fires sweep through this part of Halifax County so often that few trees ever reach maturity.

5.0   Continue STRAIGHT past a right offshoot.

5.3   At the crest of the hill you pass a stand of red pine.

> The sandy and rocky soils of this area favour the growth of **pine** of all types. You should see stands of red, white and jack pine scattered all along the trail. There's a simple way of distinguishing between the three types of pine. Whispy W-H-I-T-E (five letters) pines have needles in bunches of five while red pine are very symmetrical and have needles in bunches of two (and sometimes three). Jack pine (keep an eye out for these later) is easily distinguished by its shorter needles and twisted, gnarly appearance. In fact, pioneers used to call Jack Pine the witch's tree. These early settlers figured that Jack Pine poisoned the land because it was always found growing in such poor soil.

5.5   You've reached the beginning of Jimmy's Roundtop. Although the roundtop isn't much of a peak, you get a good view from here because the landscape is so barren. Climb up onto one of the huge erratics lining the trail for an even better view of the surrounding landscape.

> The boulder-strewn **Hubley Big Lake** lies to your left. You will probably notice huge granite boulders dotting the entire landscape. Retreating glaciers deposited these rocks twelve thousand

> years ago, during the end of our last ice age. The size
> of these monster rocks is an indication of the sheer
> magnitude and power of the glacial ice.

9.7   Cross the bridge.

10.1   Turn RIGHT at the T. This next portion of the ride follows the western end of the Old St. Margarets Bay Road.

10.2   Continue STRAIGHT past the left offshoot.

10.5   Take a peek into the small clearing on the right. Just beyond the end of the clearing you'll find an old stone wall that continues for about 50 m on both sides of the trail. It may take a few minutes to locate, but don't stray too far from the trail.

> This **stone wall** is probably a remnant from
> the mid to late 1800s when people actually cleared
> land here for sheep pasture or some subsistence
> farming. Of course the thin rocky soil made it diffi-
> cult for anything to grow. By 1865 only one land
> owner, a J. Jennings, maintained a residence here.
> He probably built the stone wall. Jennings likely
> bailed out of here after discovering that a hearty
> crop of rocks was all that this land could produce.
> The land has since reverted to the mixed forest that
> you see here today.

10.7   Cross a wooden bridge over a small brook.

14.1   Catch a brief glimpse of St. Margarets Bay off in the distance before plunging down another short rocky descents.

14.9   Make your way across a small bridge.

15.5   Continue STRAIGHT past an offshoot on the right.

15.6   Notice that the forest here is composed of much older trees with a greater mix of hardwoods. Red oak grow a little larger here due to the better soil conditions. For the rest of the ride down to Woodens Cove the trees tend to be much larger than they were back on the barrens of Jimmy's Roundtop.

16.9   Descend past a couple of old barns and a house. At the bottom of the hill there's a T intersection with a dirt road. Head LEFT and continue on the dirt road until it makes a sharp right turn onto Route 333.

17.1   Go RIGHT onto Route 333.

17.3   Cross the bridge over the Woodens River, which drains into Woodens Cove.

> John Umlah started building schooners at **Woodens Cove** in 1790. Shortly afterwards, in 1794, a family named Warrington built the first permanent dwelling in the cove. The Warrington's set up shop here to make use of the abundant oak trees. Soon after completing their home, the Warrington's followed John Umlah's lead and began building schooners from the local oak. Oak was an integral element of a schooner's hull and its scarcity in many parts of North America was a major handicap for early shipbuilders on this continent.

Make a RIGHT just past the bridge onto the Old Halifax Road. Travellers have used this route for over two hundred years. Originally a horse path to Halifax, it's mainly used nowadays by local fishermen and hunters to access inland lakes and wilderness.

Note: For the next few kilometres the trail gets rough and goes through a logging area. Some people may prefer to keep straight on Route 333 and follow the coast. It's a smoother, more scenic route. If you choose this option, follow the pavement for about 6 km more. Then turn right at Dauphinees Loop (you'll see a sign for the Old Halifax Road at the turn-off). Two hundred metres past the turn-off take another right to get onto the Old Halifax Road. Eventually (2.9 km later), you'll merge with the main trail, which enters from the right. Jump ahead to the 23.4 km mark in this guide when you rendezvous. This alternate route will add about 5 km to your day's cycling.

17.8   Keep RIGHT at the V in the trail.

18.4   You'll notice some logging activity in this area.

> **Logging** here dates back to at least the mid 1860s when fishermen turned to the land as fish stocks began to decline. By the turn of the century a local man named Steve Dauphinee built a sawmill at nearby Old Mill Pond that he powered with a water wheel. Once the trees were depleted around Old Mill Pond, Dauphinee disassembled his mill and wheel and reassembled it further inland near Croucher Lake.

19.2   Get ready for some tricky riding through a short rocky section!

20.0   On the right is a nice grassy spot looking out onto Albert Bridge Lake. This is a great place to stop for a snack or a short break.

20.2   Continue over the wooden bridge between

Brines Little Lake on the left and Albert Bridge Lake on the right.

20.9   There's a wide road heading left. Keep RIGHT.

22.7   The logging road veers left. Go STRAIGHT over the small bridge and continue on the wagon track.

23.1   Cross over a small wooden culvert. Culverts on this road date back to the days when most underground pipes were made of wood. This culvert has outlasted its expected life span by quite a few years.

23.3   Continue STRAIGHT past the offshoot on the right.

23.4   You merge with the road from Crouchers Forks. Continue STRAIGHT.

24.6   The road swings right with a sign that says "Long Lake Dr." Don't take this. Keep going STRAIGHT on the small wagon track.

24.9   Continue STRAIGHT past an offshoot on the left.

27.1   You complete the loop by meeting up with the dirt road on which you began.

27.4   The main dirt road swings left. Continue STRAIGHT onto the wagon track to return to your vehicle.

McNabs Island

Starting Point: McNabs Island is located in the mouth of Halifax Harbour. You must arrange passage through a charter boat service. Call Murphy's on the Water at (902)420-1015. The boat departs from Cable Wharf on Lower Water Street in downtown Halifax.

Length:	12.0 km
Difficulty:	easy; but still a fun ride for experienced riders
Trail Type:	wagon track and dirt road
Riding Time:	less than half a day

McNabs Island may be the most underutilized chunk of wilderness in the metropolitan Halifax area. Even though it is surrounded by a population of over 300,000, you'll probably only encounter a handful of people out on the island on any given day during the summer. Most Halifax area residents are unaware of how easy it is to get out to McNabs. This is unfortunate because it's really worth exploring. We strongly recommend forking out ten bucks to catch a boat over. With numerous trails, old military fortifications, an awesome beach and a great view of Halifax, this is one adventure you shouldn't miss.

Although the French were fishing off McNabs in the early 1600s, it wasn't until 1783 that the island received its current name. That's when Peter McNab purchased it for £1,000. The island has since gone through numerous changes in ownership. Today, the province owns most of McNabs. The southern half of the island is still owned by the federal government—a hold-over from the days when military forts on McNabs guarded the entrance to the harbour.

In addition to its military history, the island has a long tradition of recreational use. For over two centuries now, people have come to McNabs Island to have fun. Among the first were members of the local quoits club, a game similar to horseshoes. Then came Sunday picnics and social events, among them the "monster picnic" of 1845. Such events drew crowds of

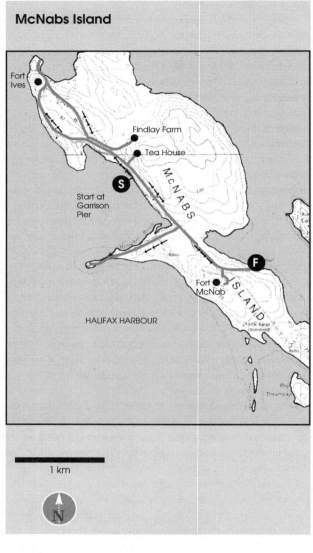

McNabs Island

Fort Ives

Findlay Farm

Tea House

S

Start at
Garrison
Pier

McNABS

F

Fort
McNab

ISLAND

HALIFAX HARBOUR

1 km

N

50 m
0
0   9.9 km

up to four thousand people and resulted in a regular ferry service to the island as early 1873.

Things have calmed down on McNabs since the days of the monster picnics, but there's still a regular ferry service to bring fun-seekers and explorers over to the island. Murphy's on the Water offer a ferry service from June to September. Their schedule depends on the demand. Call them a day or so in advance to secure a spot on the boat. The fare is $10 return. If you wish to stay overnight, bring some camping gear and arrange a pick up for the following morning. Bicycles are welcome on the boat, but call Murphy's first and let them know that you're bringing one along.

0.0   The boat docks at Garrison Pier. Reset your odometer where the pier meets the land. Begin the ride by hanging a LEFT onto Garrison Road.

> Don't be fooled by the **street names**. There are no graded roads or paved streets out here these days. The street names are left overs from a time when the island was home to fifty-five permanent residents. The only person who resides on the island now is a caretaker who works for the Nova Scotia Department of Natural Resources.

0.1   Continue STRAIGHT past an offshoot on the right.

0.4   Keep LEFT at the V in the trail.

1.1   Hugonin Battery, named after James John Hugonin, an early resident of the island, is on your right.

> The British originally built a battery here between 1899 and 1900. The Canadian Department of National Defence later took over the site and continued to operate it as a military listening post up until the end of the cold war. The military used vibration-sensitive microphones extending out under the water to monitor shipping traffic in the harbour.

1.7   Head past the caretakers residence on the right.

1.8   There's an outhouse on the right (just in case).

> **Fort Ives** is on the left. The Brits built the fort between 1865 and 1873 to protect the harbour's eastern entrance. You may want to ditch your bike and explore the ruins.
>
> You'll notice the remains of an iron fence surrounding the fort. When the fort was in active use the tops of the fence posts were razor sharp. This was to prevent the soldiers garrisoned at Fort Ives from sneaking out during the night to enjoy Halifax's night life and socializing with the ladies. But the soldiers found a way to deal with the deterrent. All they had to do was throw a mattress on the fence to cover the sharp metal. Thus, every time a group wanted to head over to the city, one soldier had to sacrifice his mattress to the cause. The next morning, of course, the guilty man's mattress would be discovered full of holes. He'd get in big trouble and be given extra duties, but such was the cost of having fun.
>
> For one poor soldier the cost was much higher, however. Having missed out when the rest of the men made their escape, this poor lad decided that, mattress or no mattress, he wasn't going to miss out on the evening's festivities. You can probably guess what happened next. The prongs later became known as "passion cures," after this soldier's unfortunate slip while attempting to jump the fence.

Only one shot was ever fired in anger from **Fort Ives**—during the late 1800s when the entire harbour was closed for military exercises. But that didn't stop a cocky American yachtsman who decided to disobey the closure and proceed into the harbour. As a joke, the men at Fort Ives decided to put a scare into the captain and crew by blasting a hole through one of the yachts sails. The skipper promptly raised the white flag and proceeded no further.

By the 1920s Fort Ives was no longer an integral part of the Halifax inner harbour defences. It continued to operate until 1943 as a training facility and barracks but ceased to have any real significance in the harbour defences.

Continue past Fort Ives down the hill to Ives Point.

1.9 Continue STRAIGHT past an offshoot on the right.

2.2 Straight out from Ives Point is a bell buoy. Just beyond this buoy is a stick extending up out of the water.

Taking a break at the tea house, McNabs Island.

> Peter McNab Jr. reported seeing a **sea serpent** at this location in 1853. Word must have gotten out about the strange sea serpent sighting as Peter was later committed to an insane asylum. The fact that the water is only eight feet deep at this location, now referred to as Ives Knoll, may have something to do with the reported sea serpent sitting. The water tends to swirl here, creating a bizarre visual effect.

Turn around and head back up the hill towards Fort Ives again.

2.6 Make a LEFT at the top of the hill onto the Old Military Road.

2.9 The two houses on the left are Conrad House and the Lynch Cottage. Both are owned and maintained by the Nova Scotia Department of Natural Resources.

> The first, **Conrad House**, was the residence of the last permanent resident on the island, Mrs. Conrad. Mrs. Conrad was the sister of Bill Lynch, of Bill Lynch Carnival Company fame. The next house on the left is the old Lynch family cottage. The small house on the right side of the Old Military Road is a private cottage that is still used seasonally.

3.1 Continue STRAIGHT past an offshoot on the right.

3.3 Head RIGHT onto the Lynch Road.

James Findlay began hosting picnics here as early as 1822. Findlay later added carnival games and a merry-go-round to his "pleasure grounds," as he called them. Bill Lynch later purchased the site and continued to use it as an amusement park until 1925. Due to declining business on the island, Lynch took the rides and games on the road and established the Bill Lynch Carnival Company. This carnival continues to tour Atlantic Canada to this day.

Exploring Fort McNab, McNabs Island.

3.7	Make a LEFT onto the Garrison Road.
3.9	Go LEFT onto the Old Military Road.
4.0	Turn RIGHT to head up towards the old Findlay Farm.
4.1	Cross over a small bridge.
4.2	The old Findlay farm is on the left. Just past the farm lie the remains of an old soda factory.

> A.J. Davis, a meat packer from Halifax, operated a distillery and **soda factory** here until 1915. Davis produced a special concoction that he called Pure McNab. Remnants of the ceramic bottles bearing this name can still be found at the site today.

Turn around and head back down to the Old Military Road.

4.4	Hang a LEFT onto the Old Military Road and then another LEFT onto the Garrison Road.
4.7	Take the road on the LEFT up to the old tea house.
4.8	Go LEFT as you head up through a small field to the tea house.
4.9	Tea house.

> John Jenkins built this quaint little tea house in 1983 and ran it as a business for ten years. The deck on the side of the tea house provides a shaded rest spot. Jenkins originally tried to run the tea house with wind power but later gave up the idea. If you take a walk up the side of Jenkins Hill, just behind the tea house, you may find the remnants of the tower Jenkins used for his failed windmill.

Head back down to the Garrison Road.

5.2   Hang a LEFT at the Garrison Road.

5.4   Just past Garrison Pier you come upon a concrete structure on the right. This was a pumphouse used in WWII to pump oil from ships in McNabs cove.

5.7   As you continue along Garrison Road you get a great view of the dune system and Mauger Beach to your right.

Both of these **coastal landforms** were formed after a road was built out to the lighthouse in the 1930s. The road prevented McNabs Cove from flushing, and created a sandy beach along its north side. It also created McNabs Pond and Hangmans Marsh.

6.0   Turn RIGHT onto the Lighthouse Road and continue out to the lighthouse.

7.2   Lighthouse

The first **lighthouse** at this spot was built in 1828 when this spit of land was still an island. You can see the foundation of an earlier lighthouse next to the new one (we're not sure if it's the original). For close to 150 years a keeper looked after the McNabs Island light, a tradition that ended in the early 1980s when the Canadian Coast Guard began automating its lighthouses. One of the more famous light keepers was "old Captain George." As a result of an accident, Captain George had to have one of his legs amputated. Not wanting to live near his buried leg, the Captain saw to it that it got buried across the harbour near York Redoubt. Years later when he passed away, the captain was buried on McNabs Island. As a result, the locals used to joke that "everyone who passes in or out of the harbour passes between the legs of old Captain George."

Before leaving the lighthouse, look out across the ocean to the south. If you started swimming south from here, the first land that you'd hit would be the coast of Antarctica, 13,685 km as the crow flies.

Head back to the Garrison Road.

8.2   Turn RIGHT.

9.0   Take the RIGHT offshoot at the top of the hill. It leads to Fort McNab.

9.1   Go RIGHT to check out the cemetery where many of the early settlers of McNabs Island are buried.

Head back out to the main trail.

9.2   Go RIGHT to reach Fort McNab.

The military constructed **Fort McNab** between 1888 and 1892. Upon completion, Fort McNab was the first fort built in Halifax to make use of breech-loading guns (as opposed to the older muzzle-loading guns that had to be loaded from the business end of the gun). In its current state, the fort has remnants of defence technology that span the decades from the 1890s up until the 1940s. The gun emplacement for the 10" breech-loading gun installed in 1892 still exists, as does the Battery Command Post built in 1941. The last major improvement to Fort McNab was the radar post, built in 1945. The radar post is still standing in the extreme southeastern corner of the fort.

After exploring Fort McNab head back out to the Garrison Road.

9.5   Go RIGHT.

9.9   The trail emerges from the woods at Back Cove. There are outhouses and a pier located here. Looking straight across Drakes Passage is Lawlor Island.

Back Cove is pretty much the end of the line. You can head to Mauger Beach and kick back until the ferry arrives or you can ditch your bicycle and continue to explore some of the more remote parts of the island on foot.

For more information on McNabs Island contact the Friends of McNabs at (902) 434-2254. This volunteer group organizes beach cleanups and helps maintain trails.

The provincial government built a quarantine station on **Lawlor Island** in 1866 to isolate cholera victims from the general population. A key proponent of the station was Sir Charles Tupper, a Halifax city health officer and Premier of Nova Scotia at the time. Tupper later became Prime Minister of Canada.

One of the more famous groups of people to be quarantined on Lawlors Island was a group of two thousand Doukhobor refugees. The government kept the Doukhobors on the island for several weeks of fumigation for smallpox. The Doukhobors were (and are) a Russian sect who take their roots from the teachings of a Russian reformist who lived in the mid-seventeenth century. They had very high moral standards, avoided drunkenness and were very hard workers. Despite all of this, they also had a bizarre side. Being doctrinaire pacifists, they avoided physical conflict. Instead, when someone really angered them, the Doukhobors would burn down their own homes while dancing around naked (or so the story goes...). Luckily, nothing went wrong in Halifax. The quarantine station escaped burning and continued to operate until 1938, when improvements in preventative health care greatly reduced the need for such a facility.

Lawrencetown Rail Trail

Starting Point: West Lawrencetown, about twenty minutes east of Dartmouth on Route 207, or via Highway 107, Exit 18. Once there, take the West Lawrencetown Road half a kilometre south of Route 207 (it starts 4 km west of Lawrencetown Beach Provincial Park). Park where the railway tracks used to cross the road.

Length:	26.2 km return
Difficulty:	easy
Trail Type:	abandoned railbed (including some singletrack!); a bit of pavement and gravel
Riding Time:	half day

This awesome coastal trip offers mountain bikers of all abilities a variety pack of great seaside attractions ranging from gentle saltmarshes to pounding surf. The route follows a section of the former Musquodoboit Railway, which served Nova Scotia's Eastern Shore between 1916 and 1980. After CN Rail abandoned the line, the provincial government snapped up the right of way to preserve it as a trail. What we've included in this tour is the only intact coastal section of the rail-line, but trail users are hoping that will change. Plans to use the railbed to connect Lawrencetown Beach with nearby Rainbow Haven Beach have been on the drawing board for several years. When the Department of Natural Resources finally replaces a couple of burnt out bridges on the Cole Harbour causeway, between the two beaches, the trail will be complete. Assuming that the Department fixes the bridges, those wanting a longer ride should consider starting at Rainbow Haven. Inquire locally for directions.

For most of this ride you stick to the railbed. In some sections the alders have grown back with a vengeance. Somehow it's hard to picture a freight train rolling through places where you've got to duck under branches and wipe leaves from your face to see where you're going. This is especially true for the inland stretches. The trail generally widens wherever it skirts the coast or cuts through marshes or sand dunes.

Our destination is the **Fishermen's Reserve.** Local fishermen who do not own property on the coast use the Reserve to access the ocean. It's as good an example of a small fishing shanty town as you'll find anywhere in Nova Scotia. To get there, we bail off the railbed around the 10 km mark and follow a local road. There are two other things worth mentioning. Don't begin the ride too late in the day. Give yourself time for a cooling off swim at Lawrencetown Beach on the way back. The beach is supervised until six o'clock. (Don't forget a bike lock if you plan to visit the beach.) Secondly, be careful on the bridges if you're not used to them. They won't collapse under your weight, but you tend to bounce around as the timbers are spaced several inches apart. You may want to *walk* your bike over some of them. There are no railings.

0.0   Head east through the bushes towards West Marsh. If you encounter any barriers on this stretch, just go around them. The entire right of way is owned by the Department of Natural Resources.

0.4   Follow the trail over West Marsh. The bridge is a good place to check out the saltmarsh.

Saltmarshes form along the sheltered spits and bays of sinking coastlines, where sediment from inland streams accumulates faster than the sea rises. This shoreline slips into the Atlantic at the rate of about one foot every century. In 1865 water covered only a tiny sliver of the present day marsh.

The saltmarsh supports a delicate balance of fresh- and saltwater plant species. The tall Spartina grass, which requires fresh water to germinate, is the most common plant here, but its dominance is kept in check by the saltwater tides that spill over from the Atlantic. The abundance of insects and small aquatic creatures in the saltmarsh makes it a hit with coastal birds (especially at low tide). Watch for a spotted sandpiper, osprey or great blue heron.

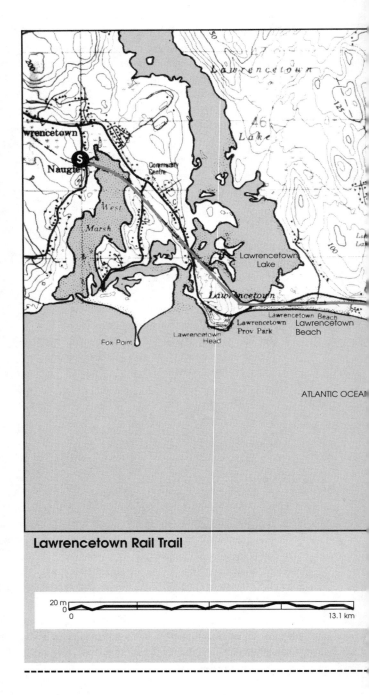

Lawrencetown Rail Trail

20 m
0

0   13.1 km

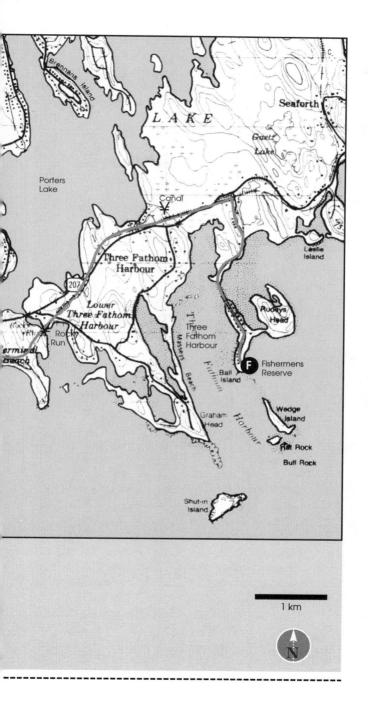

1 km

N

0.9   Continue STRAIGHT across the road.

The farmhouse on the corner is home to several horses. If you happen to encounter an equestrian, smile and be sure to yield the trail. Expect a little bit of mud for the next kilometre.

2.0   Be careful crossing this busy road.

2.2   You may want to walk this bridge. The flooded spruce trees along the periphery of this wetland provide further evidence of a submerging land. They were once high and dry.

3.2   Cross Route 207 again and enter Lawrencetown Beach Provincial Park. The railbed is now covered by a boardwalk, so follow alongside it through the parking area. Stop for some sun and surf if you can find a place to lock your bike, or wait until the way back.

Lawrencetown Beach Provincial Park appeals to everyone, from beach bums to the masses that flock here to watch the surf during offshore hurricanes. It has become a year-round mecca for local surfers. Surfers use Surfspeak lingo like "double overheads" and "a great right hand point break" to describe the conditions at Lawrencetown Beach. The beach has hosted the Canadian Surfing Championships at least four times since 1990 and continues to attract surfers from around the world. The water can be a bit chilly, but people like to swim (or at least wade) here too. The Nova Scotia Lifeguard Service supervises the beach in July and August, daily between 10:00 AM and 6:00 PM.

3.8   The boardwalk stops here. You can get back on the railbed.

> Ahead to your right is an extensive **dune system** that extends for a couple kilometres along the back of Lawrencetown Beach. Dunes are extremely fragile ecosystems, incapable of supporting bicycling or trampling. They're really just mounds of sand, pushed to the top of the beach by wind and waves, and loosely held together by American Beach Grass. Remove the grass and the dunes are history, as there would be nothing to stop the offshore winds from blowing the sand away.
>
> New dune ridges develop successively on the seaward side, as sand piles up and gets trapped by beach grass. Over time ridges flatten out due to compaction and weathering. That's why the dunes are more pronounced directly behind the beach than they are further back, near the railbed. In an undisturbed system, a more diverse collection of plant species will join the beach grass in stabilizing the dune, which will eventually support coastal white spruce and balsam fir.

4.7   Cross a private driveway.

> The trail will soon curve towards the sea around a large egg-shaped hill called a **drumlin**. These hills (there's another one anchoring the west side of Lawrencetown Beach a few kilometres back) are made up of debris dumped by retreating glaciers 12,000 years ago. Being exposed to a daily thrashing by the surf, these coastal drumlins are slowly eroding into the sea. The finer sediments get deposited on the beach and contribute to the dunes you just saw.

6.2   Pass by a bog on your left.

6.8   Cross over Rocky Run, a reversible tidal rip and popular bass fishing spot. **Caution:** This bridge is missing several cross-timbers. Be careful walking your bike across!

On the shore opposite the bridge you'll see the fishing village of **Lower Three Fathom Harbour**. Strangely enough, this cove only recently became part of the Atlantic coast. Rocky Run used to drain into a lagoon. Before the 1920s a well-developed gravel and sand bar between Half Island Point (on the right) and Graham Head cut off this inlet from the sea. But that was before the bar was extensively mined for beach stones.

In the days before crushed stone, hauling beach gravel was big business on the Eastern Shore. Around 1919 gravel trains shuttled back and forth between Dartmouth and coastal sidings every day (one of these sidings ran along the now nonexistent sand bar). With the gravel removed the land bridge gradually succumbed to the sea, and the lagoon flooded.

7.0   Head STRAIGHT across the road and into the woods.

7.9   Cross Route 207.

8.8   **Yikes!** Beware of missing bridges.

9.5   Cross over Three Fathom Harbour Canal.

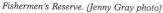

Fishermen's Reserve. (Jenny Gray photo)

Workers cut this **canal** from Porters Lake to the ocean because Rocky Run couldn't keep the lake "properly" drained. Local politicians used the canal project as a vote-buying kite for years, flown whenever they needed to polish their image. The government would call on old miners from nearby East Chezzetcook to work for up to a buck a day on the canal just prior to upcoming elections. Of course, several years passed before it was finally finished.

The government employed a similar strategy towards maintaining the railroad. They'd hire crews to replace old bridges to give the men work during tough times. This bridge, built over the canal in 1928, replaced an earlier concrete structure from 1912, which, in turn, had replaced an even earlier wooden bridge. Despite sporadic improvements along the line, the Musquodoboit Railway never reached a very high standard. The last speed limit for CN freight trains was a lame 25 mph.

10.2   Another crossing over Route 207.

10.4   Kiss the Musquodobit Railroad goodbye! Turn RIGHT onto a local road that leads to the Fishermen's Reserve.

11.9   Pass Three Fathom Harbour on your right.

Masseys Beach, across the harbour, is the home to one of the largest populations of **Canadian Geese** in Nova Scotia. In past winters people have seen up to twenty-five thousand geese at once!

12.2   Hit dirt.

12.8   Enter the Fishermen's Reserve. Cool place, huh? Watch out for cats!

13.1   Reach the end of the Reserve.

Two kilometres south of here you can see **Shut-in Island**. We dug up two short tidbits about this place. A fellow by the name of Clairmont once lived as a hermit on the island (we're not sure when). He was wanted for murder in the southern United States, so he had to keep a low profile and stayed alone on the island for several years. He pretended to be a mute so that no one would bother him (or so the story goes).

Shut-in Island probably appealed to pirates before Clairmont came along. The ground on the island is soft and spongy. That makes it a perfect place to sink your loot without leaving a trace. Furthermore, pirates didn't have to worry about eroding sand revealing their treasure. The island's coastline is solid bedrock.

When you're ready to leave, retrace your path exactly to return to the starting point. For a faster retreat take Route 207. It runs parallel to the railbed. Don't forget about the beach!

WESTERN NOVA SCOTIA

Bear River

Starting Point: The scenic look-off at Highway 101, Exit 24, in Digby County.

Length:	28.7 km
Difficulty:	moderate
Trail Type:	various standards of dirt road, lots of pavement and some wagon track
Riding Time:	full day if you hang out in Bear River for a while, long half day otherwise

Some folks call it "the little Switzerland of Nova Scotia." *Reader's Digest* recognized it as "one of Nova Scotia's unique small villages." Whatever words people use to describe Bear River, they all agree on one thing: it's a spot worth visiting. This peaceful village is neatly tucked between the banks of the river that shares its name. Beautiful old homes, churches and trees line the narrow ridge streets that run high above both sides of the river.

The area's natural beauty hasn't gone unnoticed by artists, photographers and craftspeople. They come to work in Bear River from all over Nova Scotia. Painters, sketch artists, wood carvers, potters and sculptors have all been drawn to Bear River as a source of inspiration. Samples of their work are on display (and for sale) in shops along the village's Main Street. This ride should give you a taste of what inspires this crowd. We cover both sides of the river (the Annapolis County side on the way in, the Digby County side on the way back), visit Main Street twice and explore a bit of the interior.

You may want to bring some money and a lock on this trip. The Bear River ride is the only tour in this guide where you can stop halfway and walk around something resembling a "downtown" area.

0.0   Start from the look-off parking lot and head back towards the highway.

0.1   Turn LEFT to access Highway 101. Don't go down the wrong ramp.

1.0   Cross over Bear River.

1.6   Take the Exit 23 ramp up to the RIGHT.

1.7   Near the crest of the ramp a road heads right, up a hill. Take it. Direction signs around here indicate that this road leads to the Waldeck Line.

The **Waldeck area** was settled in 1783 by soldiers returning from the American Revolution battlefield. Britain often rewarded its soldiers with land grants, but what made Waldeck different was that the soldiers were German. The Crown hired these men from the German Principality of Waldeck to fight alongside her own troops. The young Germans didn't have much choice. The Brits paid their prince for every available man he could "rent out". Exhausted after seven years of war, and having shattered most of their ties with Germany, several soldiers agreed to be part of the new Waldeck. In the mid 1780s its population peaked at a hundred. But their old lives as German soldiers hadn't prepared them for the new challenges of colonial settlers. Hampered by crop failures and unforgiving winters, most of the families left after staying in Waldeck just a few years.

As you head up the road, a peek back over your shoulder reveals a great view of the Town of Digby and the Annapolis Basin.

3.2   Take a narrow dirt road to the RIGHT.
    It's finally time to lose the pavement. The road you need begins just before a hard left turn and is the first turn-off after a yellow "60 km/h" curve sign. The dogs at this corner could spell trouble if their owners aren't around.

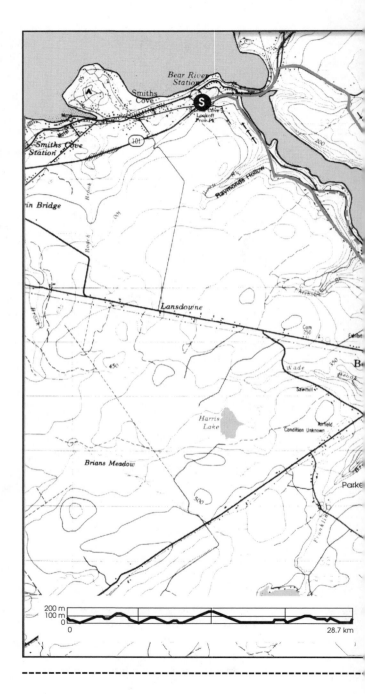

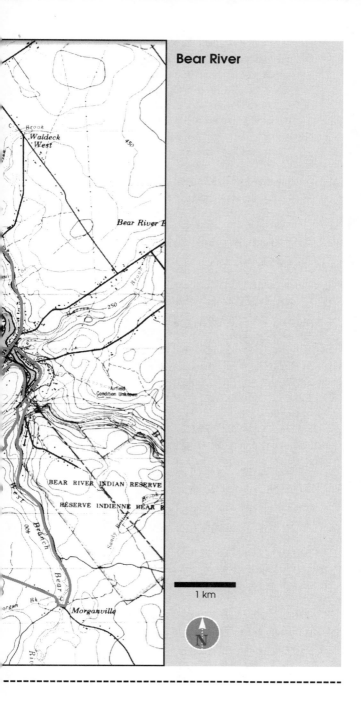

Bear River

1 km

This abandoned road to Bear River accesses old farm fields and doesn't see much action these days. You can see where the fields were located further up the road by looking for old wire fences, stone walls, fruit trees and perfectly spaced ornamental hardwoods.

3.5   Keep LEFT at the V.

4.1   On the left lies one of the many old farm fields on this road.

4.7   You start a long descent into the Kniffen Hollow grove after passing a couple of "cattle" signs.

Giant white pines, hemlocks, maples and red oaks grace the latter part of the descent. **Oak trees** on the slopes of the hollow caught the attention of a British military surveyor in 1783. Back then, the Royal Navy sent its surveyors into Nova Scotia forests to search for accessible groves of large trees, which were needed for shipbuilding. The surveyor's log described the woods between Kniffen Hollow and Bear River: "This day I did find many groves of oaks on the high ground to the east of the river, adjacent to the point of its least span. I marked by eye and stick of their heights some ten fathoms [60 ft] long and of girth a fathom round or more." Sixty years later, the Royal Navy returned to Bear River because they needed oaks to repair the *Belleisle.* This famous vessel served as a flagship in the Battle of Trafalgar. The French defeat at Trafalgar ended the Napoleonic War. Although it shared in the victory, the *Belleisle* limped away from the battle site, severely damaged. After the navy refitted the ship with Bear River oaks, it served for another fourteen years.

5.4   Pass over Kniffen Brook.

5.9   Pass a brown house on the right. Check out the Bear River below.

6.6   Turn RIGHT onto the Chute Road.

7.1   Score an excellent view of the river.

8.3   Ditto for here.

8.4   Turn RIGHT. The road leads to downtown Bear River.

8.7   Welcome to the heart of Bear River.

The Bear River, with the area's newest tourist attraction—the Solar Aquatics sewage treatment plant—in the background next to the windmill.

Since both sides of **Bear River** are built upon hillsides, the early villagers decided they needed a central (and flat!) place to erect their stores and shipyards. So they gradually filled in the sides of the river. For several years, villagers brought sleighs full of logs and granite boulders to the riverside. They eventually dumped enough fill to allow people to build where the river had previously flowed. Over time the fill has settled or decayed. That's why some of the buildings (and even the sidewalks) appear to be built on a slant.

It's probably worth your while to stop and explore this part of the village. Grab some lunch and check out the local shops. There's a Mi'kmaq craft store across the street from the war monument. They sell native art made at Eelsetkook, a nearby Indian Reserve on the West Branch Bear River. You'll find Warren Paton's toy-making studio on the wharf next to the windmill. An art gallery above the Flight of Fancy store showcases the works of several Nova Scotian artists. The store's proprietor can show you some of his renowned bird paintings on stone. He paints species that breed along Bear River, including the red-tailed hawk, belted kingfisher, osprey, bald eagle and great blue heron. Watch for these birds later on the trail.

You may also want to tour Bear River's new solar biological sewage treatment plant. You will find the plant below the windmill, built in a greenhouse. Wastewater that enters the plant is cleaned by flowing through a simulated natural wetland. The people who operate the system will be happy to show you how bacteria, fish, plants and snails break down sewage. Inquire locally for hours. This new environmental technology allows residents to enjoy a clean river without the high costs, chemicals and stench of a conventional plant. Meanwhile, the little dudes and plants who do all the work get a hearty meal every day. The Bear River "Solar Aquatics" plant is the first of its kind in Canada.

To leave the Annapolis County side of Bear River, continue STRAIGHT over the bridge.

The infilling exercise on Main Street meant that new **bridges** across the river became progressively shorter. While shorter spans could better withstand the spring ice break-up, they weren't always popular with tall ship captains. Large ships could only pass (they had swinging bridges in those days) at high tide, when the water lifted the widest part of the hull above the bridge railings. *Heritage Remembered: The Story of Bear River* recounts "an incident of faulty timing causing one ship to be caught on a falling tide, and eventually remained half suspended. The village then held its collective breath for the next eight hours, wondering which would be the first to go, the hull of the ship, held six feet above the river bed by a miscellaneous collection of logs, or the bridge structure itself". The ship survived and escaped at the next high tide.

8.8   Continue STRAIGHT at the intersection by the post office.

9.0   Go STRAIGHT.

If you're into churches or architecture, turn right. The Bear River Baptist Church is about 250 m away. The church, built in 1859, incorporates Romanesque arches and a golden cupola into its design.

9.1   Go LEFT at the V.

9.2   Take another LEFT over the falls.

The road alongside the Wade Brook gorge is typical of Bear River's narrow hillside streets. Past residents managed to make optimum use of their space on the steep riverbanks by building splendid homes. Most houses lie low to the ground in front and many are propped up by stilts in the back. Several of Bear River's older homes boast high decks that overlook the river and the rest of the village.

You can get the same view from your bike along much of this street. When you get a chance, look down on Main Street. You'll notice that space there has always been at a premium too. Several of the downtown buildings, like the Packet Restaurant (that's the big yellow one), are built directly over the river. At high tide they almost appear to be floating.

9.7   Keep RIGHT and continue following the river.

10.3   Keep STRAIGHT after crossing the West Branch Bear River.

10.4   Continue STRAIGHT past Parker Road and follow the right curve by the Gulch Hydro Plant.

10.7   Keep RIGHT at the V.

Eelsetkook, the Bear River Indian Reserve, is located up the left fork. From here the road to Morganville snakes alongside the West Branch for about 4 km. Just follow the sounds of a restless river. Local natives, many of whom live on the reserve, and their ancestors have been fishing Atlantic Salmon in this stream for centuries. Watch for the bilingual signs, written in both English and Mi'kmaq, along this road.

14.0   Fred's Hole is on the right. The locals say it's a refreshing swim spot.

14.7   RIGHT's the way to go in Morganville.

14.8   Pass over the bridge and continue STRAIGHT past the Tom Wallace Road.

16.9   Swing RIGHT onto the Parker Road.

19.5   Enjoy the descent back to the river. **Caution:** Beware of a very sharp left turn near the end of this hill. If you don't know it's coming and hit it full throttle, you're screwed. And don't forget about oncoming traffic.

20.3   Go LEFT.

20.4   Turn RIGHT. Then cross Bear River.

20.6   Keep LEFT.

21.0   Keep LEFT. Follow this road back to the village.

21.8   Enter downtown. Go LEFT.

22.0   This time go RIGHT at the intersection.

23.0   Go LEFT.
         A left turn leads to the **Riverside Road.** Its
         surface is maintained gravel (like the road to
         Morganville along the river) and it traverses
         several hills and dips. The road runs high
         above the river and thus offers some great
         views. Alternatively, you can stick to the paved
         (and flat!) road by keeping straight. Some
         cyclists prefer to mix it up by going straight
         now and then cutting up to the higher road 1
         km from here.

23.2   Hang a RIGHT onto the Riverside Road.

24.1   Go STRAIGHT. Get ready for a little climb.

24.4   You get good views of the river from this hill.

25.1   A great view to the coast rewards your climb.

25.8   Keep STRAIGHT.

27.1   Merge with the paved road. Keep LEFT.

28.2   A LEFT will bring you back to the look-off.

28.7   This should be the end.

Harbourville

Starting Point: You can park at Harbourville Hall, Harbourville, Kings County. From Highway 101, Exit 15, take Route 360 north for 12 km. The hall is on the right just after Russia Road.

Length:	26.9 km
Difficulty:	moderate
Trail Type:	various standards of dirt roads and wagon tracks; a little pavement at the start
Riding Time:	half day or less

Habourville made its debut as a tourism desti-nation long before bicycles became popular. Its loca-tion on the cool Bay of Fundy attracted rich folks from the Annapolis Valley. They used to flock to the village in the summer to escape the valley heat. The Seaside Park, Habourville's first resort hotel, went up in 1910 to accommodate the influx of visitors. By the '30s the village was rockin'. Visitors would hire local fishermen for boat tours or taxi rides, indulge at the ice-cream stands, and wrap up the day dancing at the local hall. Things have since quieted down but you'll still see sev-eral cottages, especially along the bay.

Today, Habourville makes a good destination for both mountain bikers and "roadies." You can ride very similar circuits on either paved or dirt roads. Luckily, the nicest stuff (like the steep pitches where brooks reach the coast) are still found along the dirt roads. Standards of these gravel roads range from "excellent" (i.e. wide and smooth), to "fair" (these turned out to be the most fun). Fortunately, there is more to see on the wide roads, so it all sort of evens out.

0.0   Turn RIGHT out of the Harbourville Hall parking lot and head down to the coast.

        The large island in the bay is Isle Haute, the rumoured location of several pirate treasures.

0.2   Cross over the bridge at Harbourville. Then turn RIGHT and follow the sign to Turner Brook.

Harbourville is one of only a few sheltered ports on the very straight Fundy coastline, and it's traditionally been one of the busiest. For several years, wooden cargo vessels stopped at Habourville to load up with fish, cordwood and vegetables. Some of these ships would return full of supplies for local merchants. Older residents remember the excitement when the entire village would gather at the wharf to greet the supply ships every spring. They arrived just as store shelves began to run bare.

Today you'll see a few fishing boats in the harbour. They go after scallops, lobster, herring, haddock, halibut or whatever is in season and catches the right price.

After the ride you can try some of the local catch at D & N Take-Out. They serve famous Bay of Fundy scallops.

Make a mental note of the water level as you leave Habourville. Sea level may have changed quite dramatically when you return in a few hours (10 m tides are not uncommon around here). At low tide, boats in the harbour are stranded on the dry ocean bottom.

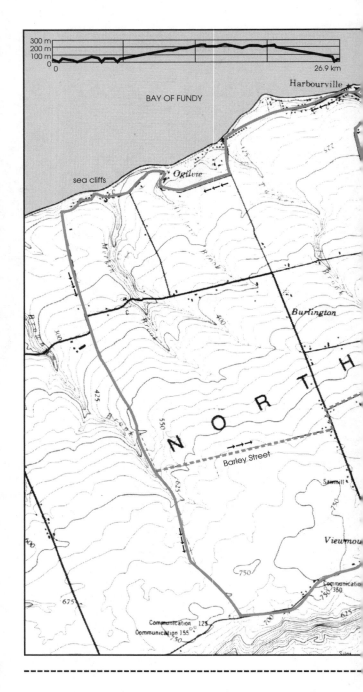

300 m
200 m
100 m
0
0
26.9 km

BAY OF FUNDY

Harbourville

sea cliffs

Ogilvie

Burlington

N O R T H

Barley Street

Sawmill

Viewmou

Communication 350

Communication 125
Communication 155

675

750

Harbourville

*A typically windy day at Harbourville,
with Isle Haute off in the distance.*

1 km

N

To explain the **Bay of Fundy's giant tides**, scientists like to use a bathtub analogy. Every body of water will, like a bathtub, slosh back and forth once it is set in motion. The water in the Bay of Fundy and Gulf of Maine just happens to slosh back and forth at approximately the same frequency as the twelve and a half hour tidal cycle. So the two forces are working together. (Nerds will recognize this phenomenon as resonance.)

The natives offer a similar explanation. One version of the story starts with the Mi'kmaq god Glooscap wanting to take a bath. But he couldn't find any water. So Glooscap called on his beaver friend to dig a trench (the Bay of Fundy). Another friend, the whale, visited Glooscap while he was bathing. So great was the amount of water displaced by these two giants that their bath created the first high tide. But when Glooscap stepped out of the bay the water began to swish back and forth, creating the giant tides.

2.6   The road takes a sharp LEFT after crossing Turner Brook.

You can walk the shoreline here for several miles at low tide. Up until a few years ago you would have seen handmade fishing weirs, spaced about a quarter mile apart, all along the coast.

3.2   Hang a RIGHT towards Ogilvie Wharf. Look back for a great view of the Bay of Fundy.

4.3   The road narrows and swings RIGHT.

4.7   Cross over Ogilvie Brook and head up the hill.

5.4   Continue STRAIGHT past the octagonal house.

5.8   Pass the Clem Family Cemetery on your right. Follow the road through a hard LEFT.

5.9   Cross over Meekin Brook.

6.1   A wooden barrier protects the road from the sea here. The cliffs along the shore to the east have been badly eroded. Cave explorers may want to take a closer look.

6.8   Keep LEFT.

8.6   Continue STRAIGHT past a well-maintained dirt road on the left.

8.8   Ignore the right curve and enter the lower standard road straight ahead. This road starts off rocky but eventually becomes smoother. Expect a few small wet spots.

A rock hound's dream. Ice working away at the cracks in this coastal cliff on the Fundy Shore near Harbourville. (Todd Wallace photo)

> Although it doesn't look too important now, this **road** used to be the main drag for the farmers who lived along it. Up until about a century ago, family farms (and the cart tracks that linked them) covered nearly all of North Mountain. Farmers used roads like this one to bring potatoes and produce to ships waiting along the bay and to markets in the valley. But with the demise of the small farm most of the lands on the mountain were abandoned. Without regular horse and cart traffic to keep the beaten path beaten, several of the main thoroughfares on North Mountain were reclaimed by the forest. Even with old maps, most are now nearly impossible to find. Yet, what remains is among the most extensive road network in the province. It was blazed long before anyone up here ever saw a car.

Except for a couple of large clearings near the beginning of this road, the rest of the old farm fields have reverted to woods. As you cycle further into the forest, look for crumbling stone walls, rusted barbed wire fences and grown-in offshoots that once marked the entrances to humble farmsteads.

11.4   Continue STRAIGHT past Barley Street. (That's the road that enters from the left.) **Note:** You can shave about five clicks from the trip by taking Barley Street but we don't recommend it. This alternate route has some messy wet spots and how you deal with the dogs at the end of the road is up to you. They may be friendly, but we didn't stick around to find out. If you do go left here, go left again at the paved road, and then immediately take the next right (the continuation of Barley Street). Jump ahead to 21.7 at the Burlington Cemetery.

12.9   The road should be in better shape by now.

If you see horseshoe tracks on the ground they're probably from Tom Daniels' two **Belgian pull horses**. When the flies aren't too bad, Tom brings his team back here to practice hauling concrete blocks. About two dozen farmers from this part of Kings County train their hauling teams on the North Mountain dirt roads. They compete at exhibitions throughout Nova Scotia. Trainers and their big horses will usually retreat to open main roads in early summer to escape the hungry black-fly armies. Tom says his horses don't mind bicycles, but these giants command respect just the same.

14.3　　Take a LEFT onto the Brow Mountain Road. Old family farms are still a dominant feature of this road.

15.1　　Score a good view down into the Annapolis Valley on the right.

Farms and orchards surround the community of **Parker Road** below. The valley, which runs for 135 km between the Minas and Annapolis Basins, generates about $125 million in farming revenue each year.

16.8　　Pass by the hanging buoy sign on the left.

The Viewmount folks brought this **buoy** here from the shore to help lost visitors. A map of the road showing the location of everyone's house is painted around its circumference.

17.0　　Cross the paved road and continue STRAIGHT along the Brow Mountain Road.

18.4　　Pass the cartwheel fence on your left.

18.8　　When you get to the Hamilton Road turn LEFT. This is another forgotten road to forgotten farms. There isn't much to see along here except old barbed wire fences erected long ago to keep livestock from escaping or getting in the way of horse-drawn carts.

21.4   Turn LEFT onto the east half of Barley Street.

21.7   Just before the cemetery go RIGHT, back onto the Hamilton Road.
Perhaps the most pleasant law of physics to the cyclist comes into play here: What goes up must come down. Time to coast to the coast! The hill provides a spectacular view of Cape Chignecto most of the way down. Follow the Hamilton Road all the way to Harbourville. Ignore any offshoots.

26.6   You can hang out in Harbourville or turn RIGHT to get back to the parking area. Notice any change in the tide level?

26.9   Back at Harbourville Hall.

Black Rock

Starting Point: The lighthouse at Black Rock Beach in Kings County. From Waterville, on Route 1 (between Highway 101, Exits 14 and 15), go north for 14 km on the Black Rock Road. The light is just a kilometre west of Canada Creek.

Length:	29.0 km
Difficulty:	moderate
Trail Type:	dirt roads and wagon tracks; some pavement
Riding Time:	half day or less

      This trip is a lot like the Harbourville tour, but it's a little more difficult as it involves more climbing. From Black Rock we'll gradually ascend past a few farms on the north face of North Mountain. Nothing too serious here; it's only a 180 m climb on a wide dirt road. Then we'll plummet down the mountain's steep southern escarpment into the Annapolis Valley. After another trek back over the crest of the mountain, we coast down to the Bay of Fundy.

      North Mountain separates the Annapolis Valley from the Bay of Fundy. It's a 125 km ridge of soft sandstones capped by several layers of hardened molten lava called basalt. The ridge formed some two hundred million years ago when the great continent of Pangea started breaking apart. A rift created by the splitting crust filled with eroded sediments from surrounding uplands. Finally, molten lava broke through the shifting continental plates and coated the accumulated sandstones. This resistant basalt "blanket" has protected the mountain from the weathering power of rivers and glaciers. The southern edge of North Mountain marks the extent of lava flows. Beyond this line the unprotected sediments didn't stand a chance. They eroded away, leaving behind the Annapolis Valley.

      If you want to make a day out of your North Mountain visit, take a stroll along the rugged Black Rock beach. Start at the light. When the tide is out you can walk for miles in either direction. You'll find cliffs,

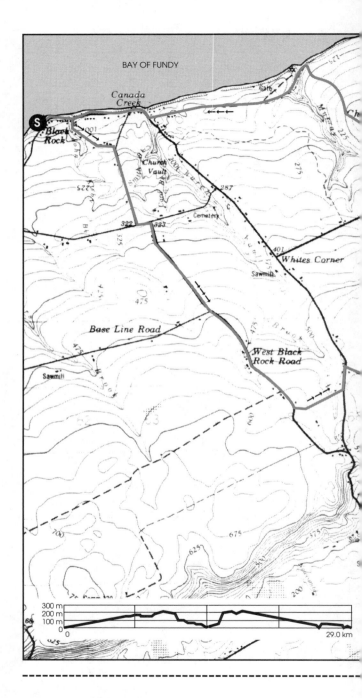

BAY OF FUNDY

Canada Creek

Black Rock

Church Vault

Cemetery

Whites Corner

Sawmill

Base Line Road

West Black Rock Road

Sawmill

300 m		
200 m		
100 m		
0		29.0 km

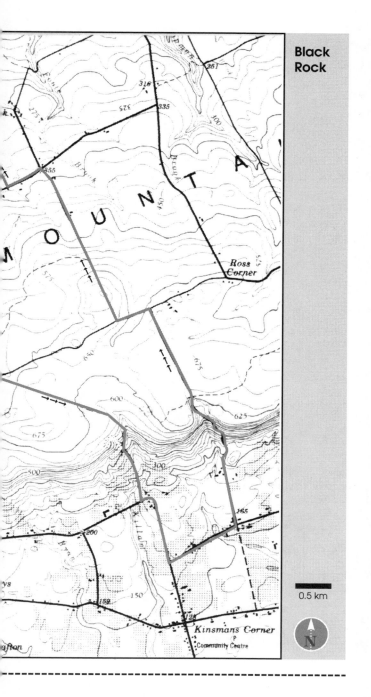

Black
Rock

0.5 km

N

caves, driftwood, waterfalls, pillow lavas (rounded mounds of hardened lava that escaped through the ancient sea floor) and a variety of marine life, ranging from periwinkles and conch shells to edible mussels and sea urchins. Check tide pools for trapped sea creatures. You'll find pools wherever cracks and depressions in the bedrock capture seawater.

Amateur rock collectors enjoy combing the Fundy shore for agate, amethyst and zeolites. Ice that forms in cracks of the cliffs every winter forces previously inaccessible pieces of these rocks to fall to the beach. Thus rock hounds can expect to find a new supply of collectibles every spring. Again, the Black Rock beach is a good place to look.

0.0   Reset your odometer where the driveway to the light meets the main dirt road. Turn LEFT.

0.4   Continue STRAIGHT after a sharp right curve in the road.

1.2   Turn RIGHT.

2.5   Hang a LEFT.

2.7   And then a RIGHT.

3.4   Pass the Calkins' big blue mailbox on your right.

4.3   Continue STRAIGHT past the Baseline Road.

5.3   Pass by the sheep farm on the right.

6.3   Hang a LEFT onto a lower standard road.

7.2   Take a LEFT at the paved road.

7.6   Turn RIGHT onto the Hiltz Road.

8.6   A narrow opening heads diagonally into the

woods here on the RIGHT. Take it. (Finally, a *real* trail!) It leads to the Annapolis Valley. This cart track is a long-forgotten Department of Transportation right of way that no one needed after the Province improved and paved other roads on the mountainside. You'll get some shade on this next part, but the bugs can be brutal.

10.3 Take a run at "The Soup."

10.5 Start the rocky descent down the south face of the North Mountain.

11.1 You exit the woods next to a small woodshop. There's a good view of the Annapolis Valley from here.

> The opposite side of the valley is bounded by **South Mountain**, part of a granite intrusion that extends into Yarmouth and Halifax counties. Unlike its cousin to the north, the South Mountain doesn't offer much for farming. Its soils are full of stones and the granite bedrock lies much too close to the surface. North Mountain is the younger of the two hills by about two hundred million years.

12.0 Turn LEFT.

Departing the parking area near the light at Black Rock.

There are a few kilometres of pavement
before heading back up the mountain.

12.3   Pass the Bligh Farm on your right.

> This is **orchard country**. The Acadians
> started planting apple trees in the Annapolis Valley
> long before the British expelled most of them in
> 1755. Under the third generation of "replacement"
> English planters, the fruit industry boomed. By the
> 1860s fruit growers were shipping massive quanti-
> ties of apples to England to satisfy the appetites of
> hungry Londoners. According to the Blomidon
> Naturalists Society, the apple barrel was a Nova
> Scotian invention, first constructed by Daniel
> O'Neil of New Ross in 1863. The early coopers had
> to work quickly. In peak years, they built over 1.5
> million barrels to meet England's demand for
> delicious valley apples. Today, apple and juice sales
> contribute about $11 million to the valley's
> economy each year. Communities throughout the
> Annapolis Valley celebrate the Apple Blossom
> Festival during the last week of May. Inquire locally
> for a schedule of events.

13.2   Turn LEFT at the Woodville Road.

13.6   Pass the Foote Family Farm.

14.3   Hang a LEFT onto the Burgess Mountain
           Road.

15.4   The pavement ends. A 115 m climb begins.

15.8   If you need to take a break, stop here. Turn
           around for an excellent view of the valley.

18.0   Turn LEFT when you meet the Hiltz Road
           again.

18.5   Take a RIGHT.

19.0   At 205 m above the sea, this is the highest
point of the ride. You can see Cape d'Or
straight across the Minas Channel.

> It's no coincidence that the road appears to
> make a beeline for the cape. Early road builders on
> North Mountain needed a landmark to head for
> when they blazed the original trail. The trail blazers
> sometimes got help from the sounds of a conch
> shell horn. Oldtimers claim that a horn player
> would sail across the bay and blow his shell from
> the edge of Cape d'Or. That way, even if the land-
> mark wasn't in sight, workers could still cut a path
> towards the sound. For this reason, several roads on
> the North Mountain used to be referred to as
> **"Conch Shell Roads."**

20.2   Ignore the arrow and offshoot on the right.
Keep STRAIGHT.

21.2   Turn LEFT at the intersection.

22.7   Hang a RIGHT across from Murray Doherty's
mailbox.

24.5   There's a sharp LEFT here where Murray
Brook drains into the Minas Channel.

24.8   Cross the bridge.

25.4   Continue STRAIGHT at the tiny clearing. The
road to the right leads to a lighthouse, but the
gate is usually locked.

27.3   Turn RIGHT at the paved road.

27.6   Pass the Canada Creek government wharf.

28.3   There's a break in the trees here, so you can

finally get a decent view across the channel. Cape Chignecto is the furthest point west. To its right, from west to east, are Advocate Bay, Cape d'Or (the nearest point on the other side), Cape Spencer and Spencers Island. Because these cliffs tower so high above the water, the opposite coast appears to be just a stone's throw away. Cape Spencer and Canada Creek are actually 16 km apart.

According to Mi'kmaq legend, **Spencers Island** was created after one of Glooscap's moose hunts. After boiling moose bones at a beach on the opposite shore, the natives' god threw his kettle into the bay. The kettle formed an island when it landed upside down with its bottom sticking out of the water.

Unfortunately, the view is often obscured or completely wiped out by **fog**. The chilly water of the Bay of Fundy causes moist warm air blowing over North Mountain to cool and condense. The cold water, fog and offshore breezes often create miserable weather for those living along the Fundy coast. On any given day, however, people in communities just a few kilometres further inland may be roasting in sunshine and temperatures up to ten degrees higher.

28.6   Veer RIGHT here.

Check out the wood carvings on the lawn of the white house at the corner. That fisherman's wearing a Sou'wester, the perfect hat to combat the bay's driving rains.

29.0   The turn-off to the Black Rock light marks the end of a day's cycling.

CUMBERLAND & COLCHESTER COUNTIES

OLD BARNS

Starting Point: The junction of Route 236 and the Windsor-Truro Road in Old Barns, Colchester County. There's a United Church near the intersection. From the Truro side go 7 km west of Highway 102, Exit 14.

Length:	30.0 km
Difficulty:	easy to moderate
Trail Type:	mostly wide dirt roads, with 4 km of wagon track that you do twice
Riding Time:	half day

This ride passes through quiet rolling farmlands near the head of Cobequid Bay. Follow uncrowded dirt roads past expansive dairy farms and Acadian dyke-lands to the red cliffs of the Shubenacadie River and the world's highest tides. Because farming has opened up most of this landscape, we'll score some good views of both the river and the bay, with its tidal flats and the Cobequid Hills in the background. The prized farm-land in the region is no match for the tides, as the tidal Shubenacadie and Salmon Rivers churn out hundreds of tonnes of sediment annually.

Trees have reclaimed the abandoned farmland between Black Rock and Princeport, so the old road between these two points has been reduced to a narrow wagon track. This stretch offers a change of scenery and some slightly more interesting riding terrain. **Note:** Part of this old road cuts straight through a hunting "preserve," so stay clear of this tour in the fall.

0.0   Head up the Truro-Windsor Road through Old Barns.

> **Old Barns** was originally settled by French Acadians in 1714. The French later fled the area under British threat, and British immigrants soon claimed the land for themselves. The locals began to refer to the area as Old Barns around 1784. The reference was to a couple of old barns that the French left standing in their rush to leave the area. The barns were eventually torn down in the 1820s but the name stuck. Now there's a new generation of old barns to take their place. Most of the barns around here now house dairy cows.

0.4   The dykes far off to the right were built over the sites of original Acadian dykes.

2.7   Before the gradual downhill here, you get a good view on the right of the Cobequid Hills across the bay. (Try the Castlereagh trip for a challenging ride into the Cobequids.)

4.0   Turn LEFT, bypassing the Henderson Road.

4.6   Hit a T intersection with the Black Rock Road. Go RIGHT.

7.0   Straight ahead, the village of Maitland sits atop the cliffs on the other side of the Shubenacadie River.

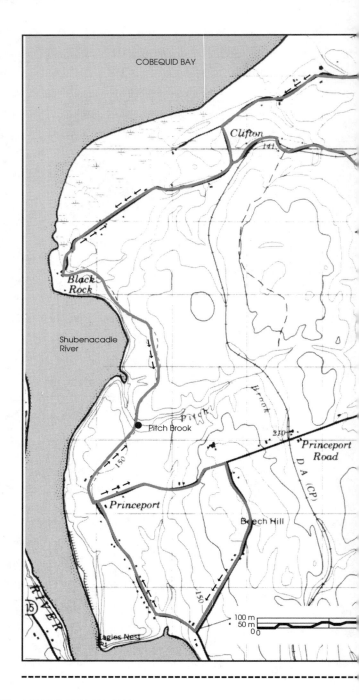

COBEQUID BAY

Clifton

141

Black Rock

Shubenacadie River

Pitch Brook

Pitch *Brook*

Brook

210

Princeport Road

150

D A (CP)

Princeport

B ech Hill

150

RIVER

15

gles Nest

100 m
50 m
0 0

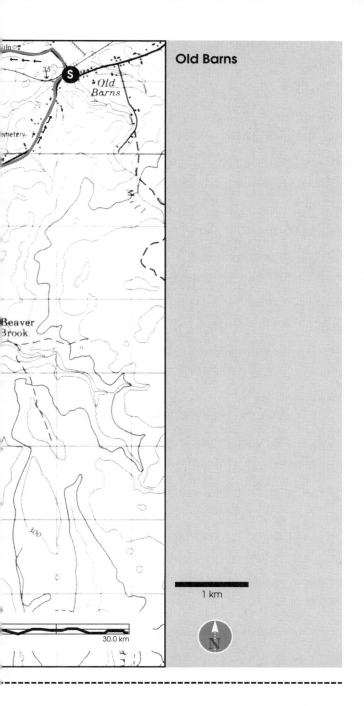

Old Barns

Old
Barns

Beaver
Brook

100

1 km

30.0 km

N

Like so many other coastal Nova Scotia villages, **Maitland** prospered in the late 1800s during the golden age of sail, or what many historians refer to as "the age of wooden ships and iron men." On October 27, 1874, William D. Lawrence launched Canada's largest ever wooden ship from Maitland's shore into Cobequid Bay. Lawrence figured he could make more money running "one ship the size of two ships, but needing just one crew". The "Big Ship," as locals called it, was a 244 ft. x 80 ft. three-masted square rigger. (Square riggers have square sails and look like the pirate ships from the movies) Lawrence used 8,000 sq. yds. of canvas for the sails, and 200 tons of bolts kept the whole thing together. The Nova Scotia Museum Complex now operates an exhibition on the "Big Ship" and the Maitland Area out of Lawrence's former home.

7.4   Welcome to Black Rock, at the mouth of the Shubenacadie River.

Samuel Creelman and his family were the first people to settle in Black Rock in 1772. The Creelmans owned the land all the way south to Princeport, where the sons later settled. The wagon track on the left will take you through these lands to Princeport. Much of the old farmland has reverted to forest.

Robert and William Forbes operated a **ferry service** across the mouth of the Shubenacadie River from here prior to 1811. This service continued to be offered by a number of other operators up until 1934. Ferries could not operate at low tide as there wasn't any water. The Maitland church, careful to ensure a full house, scheduled its services to suit the tide. The church elders must have grown tired of the ol' "the tide was too low" excuse.

Turn LEFT onto a wagon track, just before the farm. Please respect the private property on either side of this road.

To get a better view of "The Mouth," take a quick spin up towards the white farmhouse. Turn off your odometre.

Before you go, make a mental note of the tide level. Compare this with how much higher (or lower) the tide is when you pass by here again on the way back. Every twelve and a half hours a wall of seawater called a **tidal bore** begins to build as the incoming tide charges up the river. Unfortunately, the tidal bore is difficult to appreciate on a bicycle (although you can give it a try!). Bill MacKay offers a 3 hour/30 km rafting adventure on the bore nearly every day. Call (902) 752-0899 for more information.

8.3 A long hill starts here. Watch for spring-loaded alders if you're travelling single file in a group!

10.2 Slow down! **Caution:** The bridge is out at Pitch Brook.

10.6 Continue STRAIGHT past the offshoot on the left. You'll notice "NO TRESPASSING REGULATED HUNTING PRESERVE" signs on both sides of the right of way. (You'd better split if you're out here in the middle of November.) Wouldn't hurt to tuck in those white T-shirts just the same.

10.7 You emerge from the woods next to a farmer's field. Keep RIGHT along the edge of the woods. This is the Department of Transportation right of way. As a courtesy to the landowner, please stay off the field even though it may seem like an easier route.

11.2 Continue past the farmhouse on your right. This family owns a loud dog. It was in a cage when we went through, but be on the lookout. Don't underestimate the loose chickens either.

11.5   Before you head onto the Princeport Road, take a look to your right.

The 45 m red cliffs on the other side of the river expose the **sandstone** that underlies this region (they may appear shorter, depending on the tide). The sandstone is easily eroded by the tidal action that has gouged this potion of the Shubenacadie River. The river carries sediment out into Cobequid Bay, which accounts for the expansive mud flats that are exposed during low tide.

Now, hang a LEFT onto the paved Princeport Road.

13.1   Turn RIGHT onto the Beech Hill Road at the top of the hill. The Froebel Institute for Early Childhood Learning is on the corner.

13.4   You get some spectacular views from up here: The hills of the western Windsor Lowlands lie off in the distance to the right. "The Mouth" and Cobequid Bay are behind you.

15.6   Turn RIGHT at the T.

16.3   Eagles Nest Point is to the left.

Several Cape Breton **bald eagles** spend their winter months along the Shubenacadie. Other bald eagles breed here and stay all year. They feed on fish stranded by the tides and poultry scraps left out by local farmers. The name isn't just for tourists; if you come here in late fall or early spring, there's an excellent chance that you'll spot one circling overhead. We did.

Behind you runs the Shubenacadie River. You can see the highway bridge and perhaps the remains of a train bridge that once crossed the river. Constructing bridges over the soft mud of the Shubenacadie has always been tricky and several men have died trying. Huge footings must be sunk deep into the mud to anchor bridge supports.

About 125 years ago, anyone with a craft narrower than the width of "twelve logs lashed together" could follow the river all the way to Halifax Harbour through the **Shubenacadie canal** system. The canal project took thirty-five years to complete, as it was continually hampered by work stoppages. When it was finished in 1861, ships entering "The Mouth" could get to Dartmouth through fifty-three miles of lakes, canals and locks. Of course, every boat had to time their entry with the tide.

18.1 Continue STRAIGHT past the Princeport Road to get back to the wagon track.

19.0 Keep LEFT at the V in the trail.

21.2 There's a good view of the Cobequid Hills and the bay here that you probably missed on the way up.

22.6 Head RIGHT onto the Black Rock Road.

25.4   Continue STRAIGHT.

26.2   Cross over the old railway crossing.

> You'll notice the Blackburn's nifty mailbox made from an old railway switch-track lever. It's a leftover from the "**Midland Railway**," built between 1898 and 1901 to connect Windsor and Truro. You should be able to see the remnants of the railbed and crossing here. Low volumes of both freight and passenger traffic required the railway to run mixed trains. Patient passengers were used to long waits while workers exchanged freight cars at several stops along the way. In 1958, the fifty-seven mile trip took two and a half hours! No need to "stop, look, listen" here anymore; the last train blew its farewell salute through these parts in the early 1980s.

28.2   Turn LEFT onto Route 236. This paved road will take you back to Old Barns.

29.9   Just before you reach the end, you'll pass the Old Barns United Church. The Reverend David Lates gives his weekly sermon every Sunday at 11:00 A.M. Remember to wipe your feet at the door.

CAPE CHIGNECTO

Starting Point: West Advocate, Cumberland County.
Head west on Route 209 from Parrsboro. Make a left
towards West Advocate, about 3 km past Advocate
Harbour. Park your vehicle at the first road on the
right, 1.2 km past the turn-off.

Length:	39.5 km
Difficulty:	easy; you can shorten the ride to 28 km and avoid pavement by turning around at Spicers Cove
Trail Type:	mainly dirt roads and wagon track; the final 16 km are paved
Riding Time:	half day

      Cape Chignecto offers incredible opportunities
for the outdoor enthusiast. Sea kayakers will find the
jagged shoreline a perfect place to explore, while tons
of old paths could keep hikers and backpackers busy
for days. For mountain bicyclists, the old Eatonville
Road from West Advocate to Spicers Cove forms the
basis of a fantastic 40 km loop. With rolling hills and
plenty of narrow wagon track, this ride is a blast.

      Before heading out, there are two things you
should consider. We didn't get a chance to find the old
lumbering village of Eatonville. Consider it your goal to
find evidence of this abandoned community.
Apparently, a set of old wooden tram tracks still lead to
the site. Secondly, if you are interested in fossil hunting
along the coast, you may wish to schedule your trip so
that you arrive at Spicers Cove during low tide. Tide
tables and information on fossils are available at the
Fundy Geological Museum in Parrsboro.

0.0	Begin the ride with about 100 m of paved road.
1.2	Continue STRAIGHT past an offshoot on the right.

Cape Chignecto

Spicer's Cove Brook.

CHIGNECTO BAY

Spicers Cove

Spicers Cove.

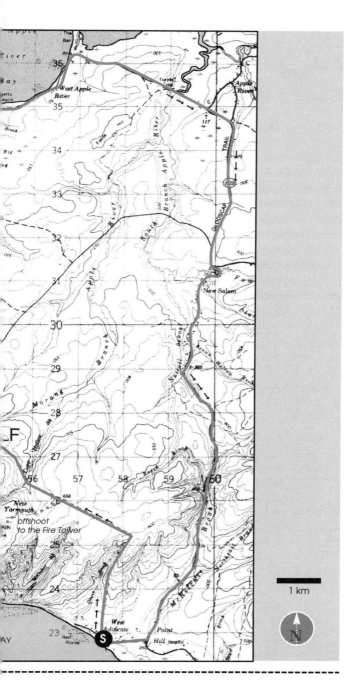

1 km

2.8   The gradual uphill ends.

3.2   Pass a house on the left.

4.4   Keep RIGHT at the V in the road.
          If you want to catch a great view, turn off your cycle computer and go left instead. After about 1 km you'll reach another V. Go left again. You'll soon come out at the **New Yarmouth fire tower**. At 275 m above sea level, this tower sits atop the highest spot on the Cape. From it you can see both the New Brunswick and Nova Scotia shores of the Bay of Fundy. Retrace your tracks (keeping right this time) to get back to the Eatonville Road.

5.0   Have fun rocketing down an overgrown tunnel-like downhill. The small stream at the bottom is Copp Hollow.

7.4   Hang on tight through this rocky downhill section.

7.9   Continue STRAIGHT through an intersection with a logging road.

10.3   Cross a small bridge.

10.2   Keep LEFT at the V in the trail. If you go right up the hill you'll end up at a private cottage.

10.5   Cross an old bridge with iron supports. **Caution:** some of the planks are rotting. Be careful.

10.6   Cross another bridge.

11.7   The field here on the right was probably part of the abandoned community known as Eatonville.

Eatonville dates back to 1864 when D. R. and F. R. Eaton began a lumbering business here. For the next eighty years Eatonville prospered, providing lumber for the nearby shipyard at Eatonville Harbour. The lumber was transported via a pole railway that consisted of trolley cars with concave wheels on log tracks. Horses pulled the cars along the tracks. In its hey day, Eatonville was a regional centre providing services for residents of Spicers Cove, New Yarmouth and West Advocate. By 1920 though, things weren't looking so good for the village. A crash in lumber prices in 1919 hit the community hard and by 1920 all but a few people left. Those that stayed earned a living collecting spruce gum, which was also used for making sealing wax. The going rate was $3 a pound. For many, this was much better than the $1 a day they had made in the lumber and shipbuilding industry. With the decline in the spruce gum business, (after all, how many of us still seal our letters with wax or chew the stuff?!) the community eventually disappeared altogether.

Apparently, some remnants of the tramway have lasted to this day. We couldn't find anything on our way through, but take a look around and see what you can find.

11.8   Bridge crossing. **Caution:** This one is dicey in spots.

12.6   Go STRAIGHT through an intersection.

12.8   Keep LEFT at the V in the trail. You should be able to see Chignecto Bay off in the distance.

13.8   Arrive at Spicers Cove. This red sandy beach seems like a great place to stop for a swim.

Spicers Cove beach rubble is littered with **fossils** dating back about 290 million years to the carboniferous era. During this era, a large inland sea known as the carboniferous basin covered much of northern and central Nova Scotia. Layers of sediment that collected over time in this basin trapped all sorts of plant and animal material. Consequently, people regularly find a wide variety of fossil types. Rock constantly falls from the top of the cliffs as waves erode the base. This exposes new fossils and results in cliffs that go beyond vertical.

Another shoreline feature are the spectacular **sea caves.** They form as the powerful Bay of Fundy tides work their way into pockets of less resistant rock. **Caution:** Be careful if you decide to explore these caves as you risk being trapped by 8 m tides. Don't even consider exploring the caves unless you have a current tide table.

Bird watchers be on the lookout! The sea cliffs are prime **Peregrine Falcon** nesting habitat. Peregrines once bred everywhere on the planet except in deserts and in tropical rain forests. This broad breeding range began to diminish by the 1960s, when Peregrines began falling victim to the pesticide DDT. Because the falcon sits atop its food chain, it began to take in large doses of DDT through its prey. Eventually, the levels became so high that the species experienced widespread reproductive failure. As a result, the Peregrine Falcon soon became an endangered species. If you are lucky enough to catch a glimpse of one here these days, you can thank a government sponsored project to release young falcons. The Canadian Wildlife Service chose this region for the project because the cliffs are a traditional nesting area. They plan to establish at least five breeding pairs.

17.7	Continue STRAIGHT past a road on the left.
18.2	Come out onto another beach.
21.2	Cross a bridge.
22.0	Pass an airfield on the right.
22.9	Beware of a nasty pooch as the dirt road turns to pavement.
24.9	Keep STRAIGHT on Route 209 East towards Advocate and New Salem.
28.4	Continue STRAIGHT.
38.3	Turn RIGHT to complete the loop towards West Advocate.
39.5	Finish the loop.

Red Rocks beach is straight down the road another 150 m or so. It's worthwhile, if you have the time, to take a stroll along the beach. The cliffs expose the western extent of the **Cobequid Fault**. One of five major faults in the province, the Cobequid Fault continues west as far as Antigonish County almost 200 km away.

Castlereagh

Starting Point: Upper Bass River, Colchester County. From the community of Bass River on Route 2, head north on the Mines Bass River Road towards Upper Bass River. (The turn off is next to the Dominion Chair Co.) Hang a sharp right at Hoegs Corner, cross the bridge and begin the ride at the start of the New Castlereagh Road on the left. It's a gravel road.

Length:	48.0 km return
Difficulty:	difficult; this ride is better suited to experienced riders
Trail Type:	dirt road and wagon track
Riding Time:	full day

This rugged full day trip takes you into the heart of the Cobequid Hills: an ancient mountain chain that stretches for 120 km across Cumberland and Colchester counties in northern Nova Scotia. Along the way you will gain an appreciation of the hardships early settlers must have faced as they attempted to establish communities in the hills, such as the one at Castlereagh. When you see how little evidence of a settlement is left, you'll have a hard time believing that people lived in this area until the early part of this century.

The route takes us past Castlereagh and Silica Lake, all the way to the top of Sugarloaf Mountain. With an elevation of just over 320 m, you will be the highest person for hundreds of kilometres. It's not quite the Rockies, but the view is spectacular.

Once you've had your fill of the view, you get to treat yourself. The final 10 km of the ride are almost entirely downhill. Keep thinking about that as you climb towards Sugarloaf Mountain.

0.0 The ride begins on a well maintained dirt road that eventually narrows into a bumpy jeep track.

2.4   Continue STRAIGHT past an offshoot on the left.

3.2   Continue STRAIGHT past an offshoot on the left.

4.9   Hang a LEFT at the T intersection as you continue to climb towards Castlereagh.

5.0   Continue STRAIGHT past a driveway on the left.

5.2   Continue STRAIGHT past an offshoot on the right.

5.6   The trees open up on the left side of the road to provide a perfect view of the serene farmland below. You have now reached the Cobequid Hills.

> The Cobequids are a raised area of land between two faults known as a fault block. Lowlands border the **Cobequid Fault Block** to the south and north. The northern fault is far less conspicuous than the Cobequid Fault in the south because it remains covered by Carboniferous deposits. The soft rocks of the lowland areas have eroded much faster than the hard metamorphic rocks of the Cobequids, exaggerating the difference between highland and lowland. Of course the last few hundred million years has been plenty of time for erosive forces to turn the one-time mountainous region into a merely hilly one.

6.8   Pass a small shack and an abandoned bus.

7.5   Continue STRAIGHT past offshoot on the right. You should be still going uphill.

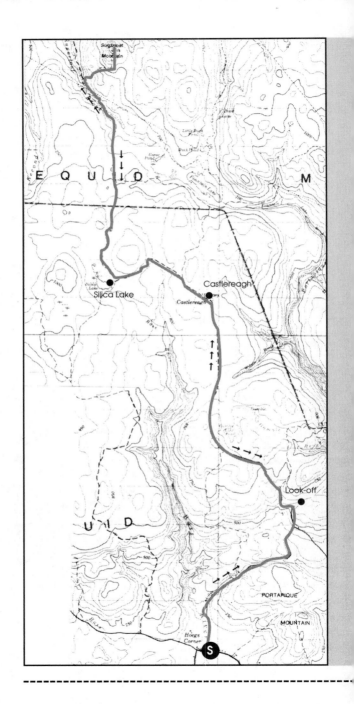

Castlereagh

1 km

Taking a break from the climb
towards Castlereagh.

7.8 Enter commercial blueberry fields. You'll see plenty of these along the way. Many of them have established over farmland that early settlers abandoned close to a century ago.

8.0 Continue STRAIGHT past an offshoot on the left.

8.6 Pass a small cabin on the left.

8.8 Continue STRAIGHT past an offshoot on the right.

9.8 Enjoy the first downhill of the ride while it lasts. There's plenty of climbing left to do.

10.8 Ignore the right offshoot. Continue STRAIGHT.

11.7 Cross over a small wooden pipe and past an offshoot on the right.

12.3 Continue STRAIGHT past an offshoot on the right.

12.4 Stop at the right offshoot. If you head in about 50 m you should find the old Castlereagh Cemetery. Some of these tombs mark the burial place of the original Irish settlers of Castlereagh in 1820. Names such as Gamble, Fulton and Staritt can be found on maps of the area dating back to 1874.

12.6 Continue STRAIGHT past an offshoot on the left and a couple of brown shacks.

12.7 Continue STRAIGHT past offshoots on the right and the left.

13.0 Head RIGHT at the V in the trail. When we were through here there was a small wooden sign on which someone had written "Silica Lake."

13.3 Continue STRAIGHT past another "Silica

Lake" sign and an offshoot on the right.

13.6 The trail splits in two. Take your pick of routes as both meet again in less than 50 m.

15.7 You've reached what the locals refer to as Silica Lake (older topographic maps done in the 1960s denote it as Bass River Lake).

Silica was discovered at the bottom of **Silica Lake** around 1890, starting a boom period for nearby Castlereagh. Not long after the discovery, an American company called the Fossil Flour Company built a mill and drained the lake to extract the silica from the bottom. The company took its name from the flourlike appearance of processed silica. Fossil Flour transported 100 lb. bags of silica to Bass River via a pole railway that they constructed in 1895. From Bass River the silica was shipped to the United States where it was used to produce glass.

A mysterious fire later destroyed the Fossil Flour Company's mill at Silica Lake. Shortly after, a couple of fellows from Oxford, Nova Scotia, bought the business. They couldn't manage to turn a profit with their much smaller operation and ended up moving to Tatamagouche.

There wasn't much left of Silica Lake once the mining ceased. Afterall, the lake had to be drained to get at the silica. Fortunately, nature was able to remedy the situation. In the end, beaver dams helped reverse much of the damage done by the mining operation. By the 1950s the lake had rejuvenated, and to this day it continues to be a popular fishing spot.

16.0 Continue STRAIGHT past an offshoot on the left.

18.6 Continue STRAIGHT past an offshoot on the left.

18.9 Continue STRAIGHT past an offshoot on the right.

21.0   Take a breather. There's a great little swimming hole to the right of the bridge.

21.2   Head LEFT at the V in the trail.

21.5   Cross the bridge.

22.3   Make a RIGHT to begin the gruelling 2 km climb to the fire tower. There's nothing to see on the ride up, but the view from the tower is a beauty.

24.0   Now you can give your legs a rest! Catch your breath and then check out the fire tower and the view.

Since this ride is point-to-point and not a loop, you get to rocket down that miserable hill and coast back to the Mines Bass River Road. Enjoy the ride!

Our thanks to John LeDuc for suggesting this trail.

Swoosh . . . having a blast in the puddles before the death march up Sugarloaf Mountain.

EASTERN MAINLAND

Eigg Mountain

Starting Point: Arisaig Provincial Park on Route 245 in Antigonish County.

Length:	25.0 km
Difficulty:	moderate; the first 7 km are uphill, but the climb is very gradual
Trail Type:	wagon track up Doctors Brook gorge and then a mix of rocky logging roads, wagon track and pavement back
Riding Time:	half day

This ride into the Pictou-Antigonish Highlands is a bit like four rides in one. We begin by snaking up alongside the clean and cool water of Doctors Brook (great place to shoot a beer ad!) in a picturesque ravine shaded by towering hardwoods. Then, whammo! Everything becomes very rectilinear and "organized" as we hit the plateau. Up here the cyclist follows straight and level roads past square blocks of perfectly spaced young spruce. Sunscreen is a must; the tree farms don't shelter the traveller nearly as well as the majestic hardwoods they replaced. The plateau offers spectacular views of Prince Edward Island and the Northumberland Strait. Gravity does the work on the slalomlike run back down the mountain and through the old hemlocks that grace Knoydart Brook. The ride ends with an easy stretch on Route 245, an uncrowded paved road along the scenic Northumberland Strait.

This trip offers a remote setting, but we'll be riding where others have come and gone. The first settlers on Eigg Mountain were emigrants from the Isle of Eigg on the west coast of the Scottish highlands. During the late 1800s, six families lived up on the mountain, most of them farmers. At that time a trip across the plateau would take you through modest farm fields marked by huge stone cairns and past a schoolhouse built for the local children. Today things are much different. No physical evidence exists to suggest that anyone has ever lived up here.

This doesn't mean that you won't see the

impact humans have had on the landscape though. Much of the magnificent northern deciduous forest that greeted the early settlers, and continued to flourish long after they left, is methodically being replaced by monoculture spruce plantations. This is especially true on the plateau where the provincial government leases crown land for silvaculture. (Luckily, enough hardwoods still thrive on the lower stretches of the trail to make this ride a scenic choice, especially in the fall.)

On a more humorous note, there's the work of old Vincent MacDonald. Vincent was the farmer turned would-be water baron who tried busting open the floodgates to his pocketbook with an ingenious scheme to sell mountain runoff to the thirsty folks down in Antigonish. Today his unfinished canal system rots away up on the plateau. While the ill-fated project never gave Vincent cause to celebrate, the local spring peepers certainly aren't complaining about what he left behind. The frogs that moved into Vincent's ditches hold a boisterous party in his honour following each year's spring thaw. If you miss the fall colours on this ride, maybe you'll at least be around when the peeper party hits full swing in early May. Before then, snow will render much of this ride impassable.

0.0   Leave Arisaig Provincial Park and head RIGHT onto Route 245.

0.2   Continue STRAIGHT past the first dirt road on the left.

0.3   Turn LEFT onto the MacDonald Road.

0.9   Things may appear a little darker as you enter a steep chasm. The slopes of this hollow expose the soft sedimentary bedrock that, over time, has been no match for the brook's erosive power. As you make your way up the mountain, the underlying bedrock will become progressively older and harder.

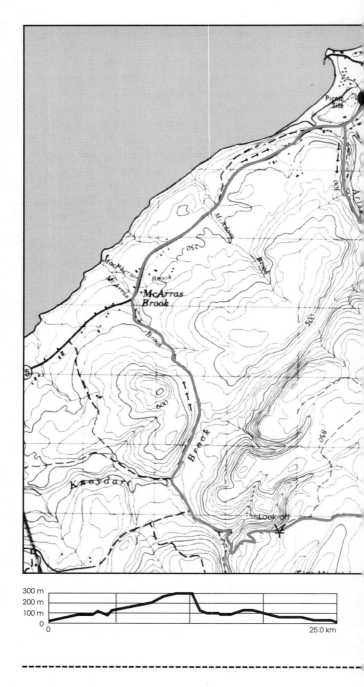

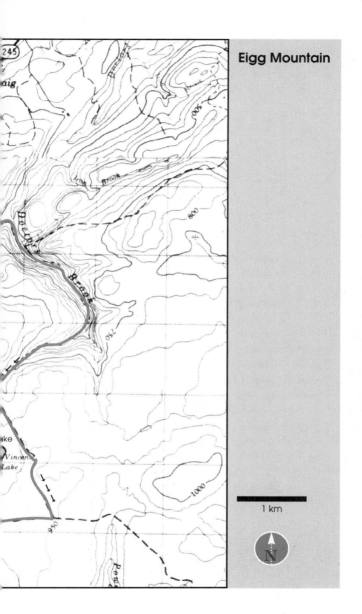

Eigg Mountain

1 km

N

1.0   Cross back over Arisaig Brook.

2.3   Pass a house on the left. Then continue
STRAIGHT past a right offshoot.

2.5   Pooch alert on the left.

2.7   Ignore the left offshoot. Go STRAIGHT.

3.2   Here you cross into the Pictou-Antigonish
Highlands. This 1,500 km^2 mound of largely
600-million-year-old Precambrian rock underlies much of both Antigonish and Pictou
counties. The Highlands are part of the
Appalacian Mountain Range, which extends
south to Georgia.

3.6   After crossing Doctors Brook go RIGHT at
the V.

Tattered maps tucked away at the
Department of Transportation office in Halifax list
this route as the **"Old Trunk Road,"** but it was
probably never a major thoroughfare. Today, it
appears to be a popular snowmobile path (judging
by the abandoned machines further up the trail) as
well as a scenic bicycle trail. The wagon track follows Doctors Brook for about 3 km.

For those who enjoy the outdoors, the
chance to immerse themselves in a hardwood forest
is still quite a treat. While spruce and balsam fir
manage to grow on the flat river banks, the rocky
and rapidly draining hillsides along this gorge
favour birches and maples. People have selectively
cut along this road for generations without inflicting
major changes to the forest composition. Back in
1875 a sawmill operated near here.

4.7   Keep STRAIGHT. Ignore the path that goes
right, over the brook.

5.2   Be very careful crossing the brook. **Note:** If you use the rickety bridge, be sure to walk it.

7.1   You hit a T intersection with a well-maintained logging road. Go LEFT. Now would be a good time for more sunscreen.

7.2   Continue STRAIGHT past an offshoot on the left.

7.9   Continue STRAIGHT past the K. Teasdale Road.

9.2   You reach a T intersection with another well maintained logging road. Head RIGHT.

A left turn here a hundred years ago would have brought you into the tiny community of Maple Ridge. It's not hard to tell where the name came from.

10.1   Continue STRAIGHT past a road that heads left.

A cut through the trees at one o'clock offers a view of Prince Edward Island 35 km offshore.

The Pictou-Antigonish Highlands and parts of Cape Breton represent the northeastern limit of the continent's northern deciduous forest. On a mountain ridge ahead to the left you'll see a remnant of the **sugar maple–yellow birch–beech forest** that once also dominated this plateau. That's quite a difference from the "managed" forest growing on both sides of this road now. This type of conversion is typical of what's happening to many of Nova Scotia's native hardwood stands.

10.6   Take the first RIGHT immediately after crossing the small canal that Vincent MacDonald built in the 1950s. This wagon track to

Vincents Lake is a worthwhile sidetrip to a secluded rest stop.

11.1   Continue STRAIGHT past a left offshoot.

11.7   The raised grassy area where the canal meets the lake is a good place to stop. Check out what's left of Vincent's control gate!

Vincent MacDonald's idea was to capitalize on the inadequacies of Antigonish's old reservoir, which often went dry during the hot summer months. When the town called for his help, he would rip open this gate (at least, that was the plan). Water would then rush through the canal down to the Rights River and eventually fill the empty reservoir (the lake's natural drainage is north, to the strait). Of course no one digs for free and old Vincent intended to charge a hefty fee for his services. Unfortunately the town wasn't buying into his scheme and as a result he never made a penny from it. In 1978 Antigonish built a new reservoir on the James River.

The canal is now a rich breeding ground for aquatic insects and amphibians. In late April the spring peepers thaw out and make no mistake about advertising it to the world!

When you're finished exploring the lake, retrace your treads back to the main road.

12.8   Go RIGHT when you return to the main road.

13.9   Go STRAIGHT.

14.1   Continue STRAIGHT. The offshoot on the left- leads towards the peak of Eigg Mountain.

In 1875 a farmer by the name of Fraser was actually living up there. At that time you would have passed by six small farms and a schoolhouse by now.

14.3 Keep an eye out for a spectacular look-off point on the right.

> This spot provides a fantastic view of **Knoydart Hollow** and the ocean off in the distance. The soft sedimentary bedrock doesn't offer much resistance to the carving action of mountain rivers. Consequently, deep valleys like this one are common along the margins of the Pictou-Antigonish Highlands.
>
> Beyond the valley you can see mainland Pictou County (far left), Pictou Island (centre) and Prince Edward Island (off to the right).
>
> One final note about this spot: It's a darn good place for echoes (a three-second response is child's play; five's a little more challenging). But don't get carried away! This tranquil perch is at its finest when the only sounds are those coming from the wind, water and wild creatures.

Now, hold onto your helmets for one heck of a twisting descent down the northwest side of Eigg Mountain. Vehicles still use this route so be on the lookout for oncoming traffic. And if you overshoot one of the curves, please let us know if the valley does indeed have a bottom.

15.9 Cross Knoydart Brook and follow the trail as it curves left. This brook used to drain Knoydart Lake (now known as Vincents Lake).

16.7 Keep going STRAIGHT past the bridge on the left. You should stick to this main dirt road all the way to Route 245.

The road over the bridge leads to Dunma-glass, another abandoned mountain community. Most of the other offshoots between here and Route 245 lead to abandoned farmsteads.

17.2   Cross Knoydart Brook again.

17.5   As you grind up this gradual hill take a second to look down at the road.

> The gravel on the trail, as well as the rock exposed along the road cut, is a reddish purple colour. Geologists believe that these layers of **rock** were sediments deposited on the coastal flood plain of a large river that once flowed here about four hundred million years ago when Nova Scotia was part of the supercontinent, Panagea.

20.0   Hang a RIGHT onto Route 245 and take the Sunrise Trail back to the Provincial Park.

25.0   The ride finishes where it began.

For relaxing **apres-bike** activities, consider a visit to the park's waterfall or a leisurely hunt for fossils along its beach. If you're heading to Antigonish with a few minutes to spare, we recommend taking Route 337 around Cape George. Some locals refer to it as the "mini Cabot Trail" due to its similarity to the famed route around Cape Breton. It's out of the way, but definitely worth visiting.

Guysborough

Starting Point: A couple hundred metres past the turn-off to Larry's River on Route 16, 3 km south of Guysborough, Guysborough County. You can park at Mead's Irving.

Length:	24.7 km
Difficulty:	difficult, only because of the climb to the firetower (the rest is a breeze)
Trail Type:	abandoned railbed, rocky dirt roads and a lot of pavement to make connections
Riding Time:	half day; or skip the fire tower climb and do the lower loop in an hour or two

It was July 1931. At the end of another back-breaking day working on Guysborough Railway, the foreman told Errington Cooke not to bother showing up for work the next morning. Errington, who now lives near Goshen, was sixteen at the time and was probably preparing to return to the workers' camp. But the new Conservative government in Ottawa had finally killed the project. The next day an errie silence replaced the familiar sounds that people in Guysborough County had grown accustomed to: sledgehammers and dynamite. Errington Cooke and two thousand other men began looking for new jobs that day.

The story of the Guysborough Railway would be comical if it hadn't thrown so many men out of work. The project was a political football from the start, constantly fumbled by successive federal governments. Wilfred Laurier's Liberal administration called for construction tenders in August 1911, apparently to influence the local vote in the upcoming general election. Guysborough voters sent a Liberal MP to Ottawa, but the Tories won nationally. You could forget about the Conservatives handing out patronage in a Liberal riding —they killed the project. The Grits returned to power in 1921, and between 1923 and 1925 the House of Commons passed three bills to commence the project but each attempt was torpedoed by the Tory-dominated Senate. Finally, in 1929, the feds hired a Toronto com-

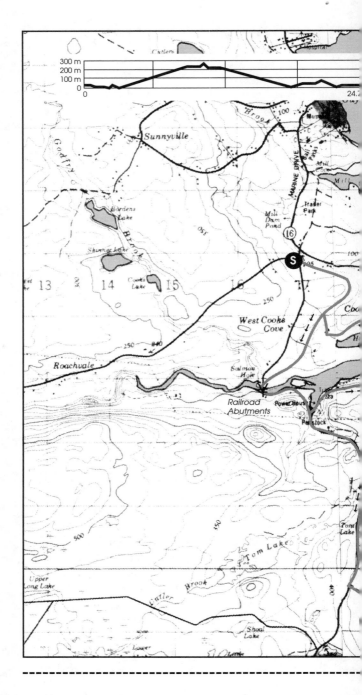

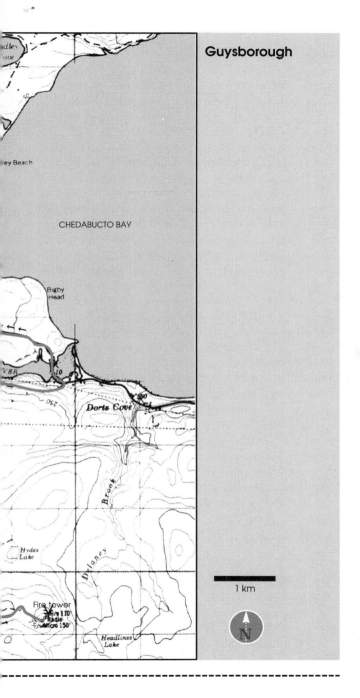

Guysborough

CHEDABUCTO BAY

ley Beach

Bigby
Head

V8R

Dorts Cove

Brook

Hydes
Lake

Delaney

Fire tower

Headlines
Lake

1 km

N

pany to begin building the railroad. By this time both Houses were under Liberal control. Construction moved ahead briskly for two years before Prime Minister Bennett's new Conservative administration canned the project for good in 1931. When Errington Cooke put in his last day, the railroad was nearly finished. Workers had already blazed a 100 km right of way to Sunnybrae, complete with most of the necessary grading, culverts and bridges. All the ties had been purchased, but the easy part, laying the track, would never get done.

While the trains never rolled into Guysborough County, we can thank people like Errington for passing on what promises to be an amazing nature trail. Within the next couple of years the railroad right of way will connect into the nearly complete Trans Canada Trail. (If all goes according to plan, the longest trail in the world will stretch from St. John's to Vancouver Island and the Arctic Ocean.) The Guysborough County Trails Association has started fixing up some nasty wet areas along the old railbed. Eventually the trail will offer several more riding opportunities. Check with the association or the local tourist bureau to find out how work is progressing and which parts of the railline you can ride (without bringing scuba gear).

We chose to include the Cooks Cove piece because, apart from offering great scenery, it's the only section that is currently free of monster wet spots. (Because it's so short we threw in the climb to the fire tower.) At publishing time this trail still had some puddles, but most were bypassed by short, singletrack detours. The trails association plans to upgrade this section.

0.0   Enter the trail across the road from Mead's Irving.

0.8   The railbed cuts across a hillside at the head of Chedabucto Bay, above Cooks Cove. On a clear day you can see Cape Breton off in the distance. Ragged Head (it looks like an island

from here) and Moose Point, to its west, jut
out from the bay's northern coastline.

About a thousand years ago, Mi'kmaq
canoeists would follow **Chedabucto Bay's** spits and
coves en route to their confederacy headquarters on
the Bras d'Or Lakes in Cape Breton. By sticking close
to land, the paddlers could duck into sheltered ponds
to wait out stormy weather.

After a possible visit from norsemen around
1000 A.D., the next Europeans to sail into the bay were
probably Portugeuse fishermen looking for a spot to
replenish depleted water casks around 1520. Between
the mid 17th and 18th centuries the bay was the
domain of French fishing vessels, protected by Fort
Chedabucto, where Guysborough now sits.

Sometime around 1768 a Massachusettes-
based fishing boat smashed into the rocks off Canso.
One of the survivors, John Cook, was rescued by
Mi'kmaq and brought to the cove that bears his name.
John, his brother Elias, and seven other pre-Loyalist
settlers eventually obtained land grants here at the
head of the bay. The newcomers enjoyed a peaceful
relationship with the natives, and the Cooks eventually learned the Mi'kmaq tongue.

The high seas beyond this cove were not so
kind. The threat of ruthless pirates faced John and
Elias every time they pulled anchor and headed out
into Chedabucto Bay. Local historian Harriet Hart
recalled the capture of John Cook by the notorious
John Paul Jones: "The pirate compelled Mr. Cook to
pilot him around the coast, and show him the way into
certain harbours, using thumbscrews and other per-
suasive powers to affect his object. [Cook] was thus
unwillingly employed for three weeks then set on
shore. Some of his adventures came to the ears of a
captain of a cutter upon the coast, and the poor man
was seized and tried as an accomplice to the celebrat-
ed sea rover. His innocence was easily proved, however, by the unanimous testimony of his neighbours."

> The early fisherman was also a farmer. Each winter saw the forest recede up the hillside to meet the colonists' demand for firewood and space for hayfields. By the time **farming** in Nova Scotia peaked in the latter part of the last century, almost all of the land at the head of the bay had been cleared. Even in the 1930s, most Cooks Cove residents maintained a livelihood of subsistence agriculture. In the meantime, forests have reclaimed the abandoned farm fields. As you head back into the woods, keep an eye out for old rock piles and stone walls amongst the trees. Rocks that interfered with horse-drawn ploughs were a nuisance to colonists and their descendants, but they sure made sturdy walls.

2.1 Cross the road that goes down to Hortons Cove.

This land, once belonging to another pre-Loyalist settler, **Isiah Horton**, bordered the Cook lands to the south. The old field in the foreground appears to be a recently abandoned hayfield and probably used to look like the active pastureland on the hill across the road. If this field is left undisturbed, young white spruce will start popping up as the land begins to revert to forest.

3.7 Turn LEFT at the paved road.

When you cross the Salmon River you'll be entering what used to be ancient Africa! About 400 million years ago the continents of ancient North America and Africa slammed into one another to create part of the supercontinent of **Panagea**. The collision and subsequent upwelling created mountains as high as the Rockies all around where you now ride. When Panagea started breaking apart 150 million years later, a small chunk of Africa stayed behind and became the southern half of Nova Scotia. The Salmon River flows along the Chedabucto Fault, which marks the division. Bedrock on the south side of the faultline is generally a couple hundred million years older than on the north.

The highly metamorphosed rock that lines the Salmon River valley to the west created some interesting challenges for railway builders. To blast a corridor through the rock, they relied on generous doses of dynamite. Farmers across the valley complained of rock fragments sailing through the sky and becoming embedded in their homes and trees. Excess rock was used to fill wet spots and build bridge supports, like the three remaining abutments that stand here as a monument to the doomed Guysborough Railway. They were built in 1930 by the Williams Brothers of Barney's River, Pictou County. When Prime Minister Bennett pulled the plug on railway construction in 1931, the workmen hadn't even had a chance to complete the span. A well-known local legend suggests that workers cemented their unpopular foreman into one of these abutments after he was murdered on the railway.

4.7   Pass the Dickie Brook Hydro Plant on the left and prepare for a 5.5 km climb. You'll stay on pavement for the first few kilometres before taking a rocky dirt road to the fire tower, which overlooks, well, just about everything.

Now if you want to skip this climb, just jump

ahead to 15.7 and take the dirt road through the hydro station. You can still drive to the fie tower later (if you don't mind cheating a bit). But we recommend continuing straight up the hill. You won't be disappointed, and coming back down is a blast!

6.0   Pass over the pipeline that supplies the power plant with water from Tom Lake.

6.3   Pass Tom Lake on your right.

8.1   A wooden sign marks the beginning of the Lundy fire tower road. Hang a LEFT.

8.5   Ignore the offshoot to the left.

As you continue your ascent you'll notice the surroundings becoming increasingly **barren and littered with boulders**. This hill is cooled molten lava. Back when the continental plates collided, the old North American crust got pushed under the denser African plate and started melting. The incredible heat and pressure forced the lava up through the overriding African plate. Most of the large hills on the south side of the fault formed the same way. Nothing grows on this windswept moonscape except for a few stunted black spruce and some low shrub plants. You may see moose up here.

10.2   Take a breather and enjoy the spectacular views!

       When you're ready, zip back down to the hydro station at Dickie Brook.

15.7   Turn RIGHT and take the dirt road past the Dickie Brook Hydro Plant.

15.8   Cross over a narrow bridge.

17.0   From up here you get a great view of Hortons Cove and, further off, Chedabucto Bay. The abandoned railbed cuts across the hill above the cove. You get back on it later, next to the white farmhouse at eight o'clock (twelve being the direction of this road). Take a quick look for circling **bald eagles** scanning the waters for food. They're common around here.

18.8   Go LEFT on Route 16.

19.2   Pass over the Salmon River.

A rockpile marks another abandoned farm field at Hortons Cove.

The **Salmon River** got its name from the French. Anyone reading explorer Nicolas Denys's account of the river would understand why, "Having gone there once to fish, I made a cast of its entrance, where it took so great a quantity of salmon that ten men could not haul it to land, and although it [the net] was new, had it not broken the salmon would have carried it off. The salmon are large; the smallest being three feet long." Denys founded the French fishing fort at Chedabucto in 1659.

The natives call the river *Anisaq*. Mi'kmaq who canoed to their headquarters on the Bras d'Or Lakes in Cape Breton entered Chedabucto Bay here. The Salmon River extends 30 km inland, where it shares a plateau with the headwaters of three other streams including the South River, flowing north to Antigonish, and the Country Harbour River, which flows southeast to the Atlantic. The St. Mary's River system, from which a paddler could access Halifax County and southwestern Nova Scotia via the Minas Basin, is also nearby. Thus the Anisaq funnelled natives from all over the mainland through this outlet on their way to Bras d'Or. People still sometimes refer to the Salmon River as the "Micmac Highway."

The importance of the river to natives was confirmed early this century when an eroding bank near the mouth of the river revealed a buried copper kettle. The pot was stuffed with human bones, a skull, hair, beads and wampum (beads used as money). Tribe members likely wrapped the dead woman's remains in fur and buried them next to the river, in a secret place safe from enemies who might treat them with disrespect.

20.9   Turn LEFT onto Hortons Cove Road.

22.6   Turn RIGHT and follow the railbed back to Mead's.

INVERNESS COUNTY

Inverness, Lake Ainslie & The Margaree

Starting Point: The Miners' Museum on Lower Water Street in Inverness.

Length: 54.4 km
Difficulty: moderate to difficult; a mix of long flat stretches and challenging hills
Trail Type: smooth abandoned railbed, lots of pavement, a few dirt roads, some wagon track
Riding Time: full day

One of the first things you notice driving through Inverness are the old wooden duplexes on Central Avenue. They are left over "red rows," built (and originally painted red) by the Inverness Railway and Coal Company at the turn of the century. The company erected about eighty of these homes to house its work force after it struck a 2 m seam of superior coal near the ocean. Shortly afterwards they built eighty more. And why not, this town was booming. In 1904 some 482 men worked in the mines. The faster these men worked, the faster the town grew. When the men reached 760 m under the Inverness coast, the town's population hovered at about 3,000. By 1906 the miners had dug down to 1,070 m. By 1909 they had hit 1,350 m. During the next few years Inverness' population peaked at nearly nine thousand, including almost one thousand miners.

The Miners' Museum on Lower Railway Street shows off the town's glory days. The museum, which operates out of the former Inverness railway station, is the starting point of this ride. We depart the old station and follow the path of Canso Strait bound coal trains along the abandoned railbed of the Inverness Railway and Coal Company. This flat and fast section is 7 km long. The remainder of the ride winds along Lake Ainslie, the Margaree River, and the county interior before rendezvousing with the spectacular coastline along Broad Cove.

For a cheap (but rustic!) place to crash while

exploring Inverness County, head to the Glenmore International Hostel on Route 395. Follow signs in Twin Rock Valley, 25 km north of Whycocomagh, 5 km south of Scotsville. Their number is (902) 258-3622, but your best bet is to just show up with a sleeping bag and ten bucks, (twelve for non-members).

Authors' Note: When we were preparing this guide, the abandoned railbed out of Inverness was still privately owned by CN Rail. However, we included it as we expect the trail to be in the public domain shortly. The Province is negotiating to purchase the right of way. The railbed may eventually become part of the Trans Canada Trail.

0.0   Begin at the Miners' Museum. Head south, behind the Cottage Workshop, and cross a paved street. The street goes to a public beach that is supervised in the summer between 10:00 A.M. & 6:00 P.M. Ahead to the right you see Inverness Harbour. It is man-made. The Broad Cove Coal Company dug it around 1890. Before the railway was built the only way to ship coal was through this artificial harbour.

0.6   Cross Route 19.

2.4   You've reached the trestle over Broad Cove River. Cross at your own risk. You may want to walk the 120 m span. Beware of the approach on the other end.

3.6   Go STRAIGHT across the Deepdale Road.

6.8   The railbed hits a paved road. Turn LEFT. The next 10 km are paved.

8.0   From here you get an excellent view of Lake Ainslie, Nova Scotia's largest natural freshwater lake.

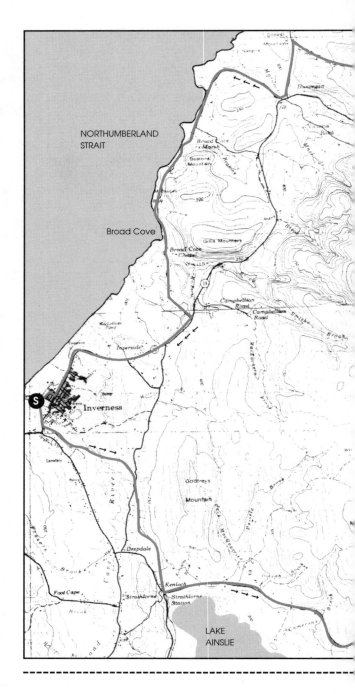

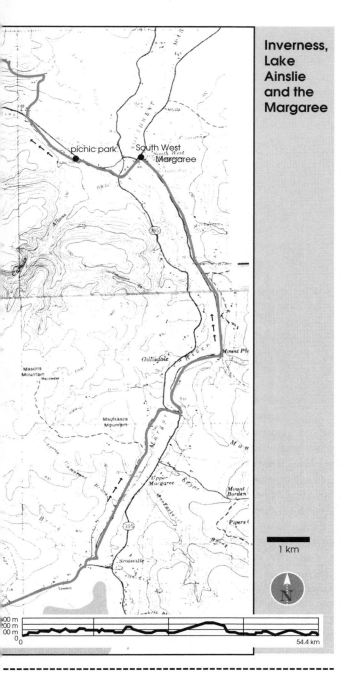

Inverness, Lake Ainslie and the Margaree

picnic park

South West Margaree

1 km

N

This road exposes you to several great views of the lake. (If you really like pavement, you can circumvent the lake on paved roads that hug Lake Ainslie's shoreline. Just turn right in Scotsville and keep the lake to your right.[Try it at night during a full moon!] It's a 53 km loop.)

> **Lake Ainslie** forms one of the headwaters of the Margaree River, a world-renowned destination for anglers. The lake also offers some excellent freshwater beaches and spectacular sunsets. We can be thankful that plans to drain the lake never materialized. Back in 1880 the provincial government offered a land grant at the *bottom* of the lake to the entrepreneurial team of Ellerhausen and Burchill. These guys wanted to drain the lake so they could drill for oil (oil had been reported at Lake Ainslie back in the 1850s and test boring began in 1864). Around the same time the government was also considering pulling the plug on Lake Ainslie to create productive farmland.

16.6   Time to lose the pavement! Turn LEFT onto a dirt road near the end of a sharp right curve (Follow the signs to WSSW Margaree and Lakeview Drive).

The only general store for miles around here is 600 m past this dirt road. There is a pop machine outside, in front of the store.

16.8   Pass over Gillis Brook.

18.5   You hit a T after crossing a bridge. Bear RIGHT and start climbing.

This ledge road runs along the Southwest Margaree River. You can see the river, which drains Lake Ainslie, from time to time through the trees.

20.0   Pass by a small clear-cut on the left.

Forestry has always been big business in Cape Breton, both for the private woodcutter and the large pulp company. Loggers have traditionally sought softwoods because they make high quality paper products, but they have recently turned to hardwoods too. Few people would lose much sleep over this small cut, but it is typical of what's happening on a larger scale throughout Inverness County. To see some *real* clear-cuts, take a spin up the Stora roads behind Pipers Glen some day (follow the road along Egypt Brook off Route 395 directly across the river from here). The annihilation of the landscape up there makes Ellerhausen and Burchill's plan to drain Lake Ainslie look like a cub scout prank. There's also a super waterfall in Pipers Glen worth checking out on your way. The early Scottish settlers used to hold bagpipe and fiddle concerts at the falls.

20.1   Pass STRAIGHT by a road on the left.

21.5   Turn RIGHT at the pavement.

21.7   Cross the Southwest Margaree River.

21.8   Turn LEFT onto a dirt road.
You're now in ESSW Margaree. At least that's what the sign says.

There seems to be a lot of **Margarees** around here. Consider this: the Southwest Margaree River passes through Upper Margaree, Southwest Southwest Margaree, and Southwest Margaree before meeting the Northeast Margaree River at Margaree Forks below Margaree Valley and Margaree Centre, and draining at Margaree Harbour after passing East Margaree. The point is, don't ask for directions to Margaree!

This road follows the Southwest Margaree
River for 8 km.

The Margaree River system (the northeast
branch flows from the Cape Breton Highlands) is
world famous for its **salmon fishing.** Atlantic
salmon swim up the river each year to reproduce.
By late autumn the lady salmon will have found a
good spawning spot, usually a gravel bed beneath
fast-flowing cold water. When the spawning ritual is
complete the salmon head back to the ocean. The
cycle repeats itself each year. Although salmon may
swim several hundred kilometres in the Atlantic
Ocean (salmon from Maritime rivers have been
caught as far away as Greenland), they always
return to their native streams. Salmon fans should
visit The Margaree Salmon Museum in Northeast
Margaree.

The Margaree River was nominated as a
Canadian Heritage River in 1991. This federal desig-
nation recognizes rivers that showcase outstanding
examples of Canada's natural heritage or offer
exceptional recreational opportunities. The
Margaree does both.

24.4 The road and the river meet again.

You've probably noticed several **weirs** by
now. There's another one here. Fishermen lower
these fish traps into the river late each spring to
cash in on the annual gaspereau run. When the
water temperature hits 10°C, the gaspereau (some
people call them kayak or alewife) charge up the
river to spawn in Lake Ainslie. The young gaspereau
generally head to sea in late summer and congregate
in offshore schools. Fishermen sell or use most of
their catch as bait.

29.5   Hit pavement. Keep LEFT of the cemetery.

29.7   Turn LEFT. Then keep STRAIGHT on Route 19 after crossing the bridge.

30.4   Keep STRAIGHT past Route 395.

31.6   Go LEFT into the picnic park.

31.9   Keep LEFT at the V by a white house and old barn.

33.2   Go STRAIGHT across Route 19.

34.2   Pass a house where hunting is *definitely* not permitted.

34.6   Make a sharp LEFT.

36.3   Check out the abandoned farmhouse on the right. It's followed by a large pile of cleared stones.

36.5   Start a well-deserved descent.

Along the Southwest Margaree River.

39.6   Go LEFT at the pavement.

40.7   Two monuments on the left mark the most famous residents of Broad Cove and Dunvegan.

Pioneer **Donald MacLeod** was the first of several Scots who hacked a homestead out of this part of the Cape Breton wilderness. MacLeod had come to Parrsboro from the Isle of Eigg in 1791. Seventeen years later he moved to Cape Breton because Parrsboro still hadn't attracted a priest. Settlers tended to be a religious lot and MacLeod feared his children would lose their faith. Although he had to leave almost everything behind, MacLeod managed to drive six head of cattle overland from Parrsboro to nearby Broad Cove Marsh. Today, a trip from Parrsboro takes nearly four hours by car!

The second monument honours **Angus L. MacDonald**, a federal politician and popular Premier of Nova Scotia for sixteen years. During World War II "Angus L." served as Canada's Minister of Defence for Naval Services. At that time Canada boasted one of the world's greatest navies with nearly five hundred warships.

41.0   Turn RIGHT onto Route 19.

41.1   Turn RIGHT again.

42.3   Pass by a campground.
          From here you get a great view of Seawolf or Margaree Island.

43.4   Pass STRAIGHT by the wharf road. Enjoy the coastal scenery!

46.2   Stop to take in the view of Sight Point, Inverness and Broad Cove.

Like most communities in Cape Breton, the settlement at **Broad Cove** started out as a quiet farming village. But that changed in 1888. That's when Massachusettes industrialist William Penn Hussey paid $62,500 for land at the cove. Hussey wanted to develop the coalfield at Broad Cove. It was among the finest coal in the world, but he had his work cut out for him. At the time, the area lacked a harbour and railroad, and local markets were nonexistant. To boot, Hussey didn't have enough money to begin mining. But where there's a will there's a way. Especially if you cheat. Ned MacDonald, the Miners's Museum curator, has recorded how Hussey used these sea cliffs to convince one wealthy capitalist to invest in his Broad Cove mining project:

"A rich manufacturer from Zurich, Switzerland, was attracted by Mr. Hussey's publicity campaign and decided to come to Broad Cove for an eye witness account. Since Hussey was one not to leave anything to chance, he hired several workers to paint walls of rock that stood facing the sea the darkest black. When the Swiss investor arrived on the scene, he looked from the deck and marvelled at the collosal black wall of coal. Such was his confidence in the scheme that he said he would be willing to invest a million dollars immediately. Without delay, the transaction was made and Hussey immersed himself in further development of the Broad Cove Mine."

By 1894 the Broad Cove Coal Company was in full swing. About a hundred men worked on building the Inverness Harbour and connecting it by rail to the coalfields. Hussey made a killing. In 1899, just five years after incorporating, the industrialist sold the mines to what would become the Inverness Railway & Coal Company. Some estimates peg his profit at a tidy $3.6 million!

48.9	Hit pavement.
49.9	Turn RIGHT. Follow Route 19 back to Inverness.
53.9	Pass the "red rows" on the right.
54.1	Hang a RIGHT at Lower Railway Street, across from Greg's Fuels.
54.4	The end.

Cape Mabou

Starting Point: Mabou Hall on Route 19 in Mabou.

Length:	36.1 km + optional sidetrips
Difficulty:	moderate to difficult
Trail Type:	wagon track, various standards of gravel road, pavement, one portage
Riding Time:	long half day

Surrounded by deep gorges, isolated coves and sea cliffs, rolling pastureland, and a calm picturesque harbour, "the Cape" is one of the most dominant fix- tures of the ceilidh countryside. It is an 8 km x 15 km knoll of very hard sedimentary and volcanic rock that rises 335 m above the Northumberland Strait between Mabou and Inverness. Luckily for us the Cape's plateau used to be littered with farms and its shores by fishing wharves and even a coal mine. The result: plen- ty of old roads and cart tracks to explore.

The ride begins at Mabou Hall on Route 19, the Ceilidh Trail. (Before we go any further some pro- nunciations are in order: It's MA-bou, not Ma-BOU, and ceilidh, a Gaelic word for "an informal gathering for music, song, and dance," is pronounced KAY-lee.) The message on the hall, "Ciad mile Failte" or "100,000 Welcomes," pretty much sums up the spirit of hospital- ity that Mabou folk have extended to visitors for as long as anyone can remember. Visitors are invited to join in weekly Celtic celebrations that showcase proud traditions handed down by the Highland Scots who set- tled the region in the early 1800s. Inquire locally to find out where to go for square dancing and the sounds of fiddles and bagpipes.

And be glad the rigid priest who served Mabou between 1865 and 1894 isn't setting the tempo anymore. This dude, Father Kenneth MacDonald, tried to confiscate every fiddle in the parish to rid the coun- tryside of the instrument's supposed "demon influ- ence." Luckily the local folks were on to him. They brought out only their second or third best fiddles if they figured Father MacDonald might crash the party.

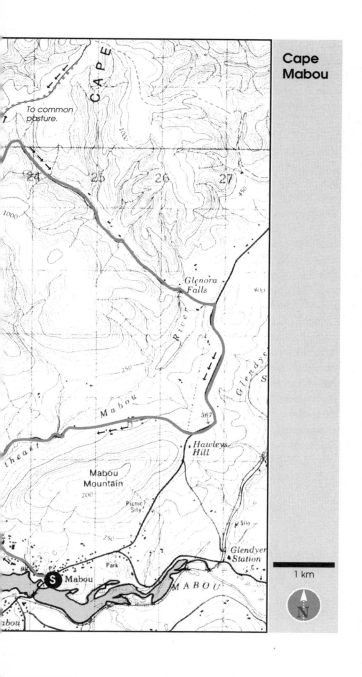

Cape
Mabou

To common
pasture.

CAPE

24 25 26 27

1000

Glenora
Falls

River

Glendye S

Mabou

367

Hawleys
Hill

theast

Mabou
Mountain
700

Picnic
Site

Silo

250

Glendyer
Station
C.

Park

S Mabou

MABOU

abou

1 km

N

So even getting busted didn't stop them from playing. MacDonald had several fiddles locked up at his house but he eventually returned them. Lucky for him no one ever figured out how to fiddle "Stairway to Heaven" backwards.

0.0   Turn LEFT out of the Mabou Hall parking lot.

0.1   Take the first RIGHT.

2.3   Cross the bridge over Northeast Cove.
        This bridge is a popular fishing spot with local kids. Check out the spectacular view across the harbour.

3.4   On the right is one of several pastures that line the slopes of the Mabou Highlands.

Early settlers modified the landscape so that it would resemble the Scottish highlands. And as in Scotland, sheep have traditionally grazed these highlands too. But you'll notice that cows have now taken their place. Sheep are harder to find around Mabou these days, a result of a consumer trend towards synthetic fabrics, competition from New Zealand and the emergence of the coyote on Cape Breton.

5.1   Continue STRAIGHT.

6.8   Turn RIGHT at the intersection.

For a quick sidetrip turn left and head down to the **public wharf** where you'll find the Mabou Harbour fishing fleet. When you're at the wharf check out the opposite side of the harbour entrance. The harbour mouth used to open a few hundred metres south of its present location. The federal government realigned the approach in 1880 to eliminate extra tacks for incoming ships.
        Today the sand dunes on the south side of the mouth are constantly shifting, according to the season.

In summer the beach is full of sand. But in the winter powerful "plunging breakers" bombard the shore. When these waves bounce off the beach they cut channels in the sand and drag sediment off to sea. The sand collects in a bar just off shore. Calm waves return the sand during the next spring and early summer.

> Don't forget to deactivate your odometer when exploring optional offshoots. This one is 0.8 km return.

7.7   Keep LEFT.

8.9   The road narrows as you pass the last house.

9.4   Stop to admire the first of several impressive views of Finlay Point and the Northumberland Strait.

Finlay Point is named after Finlay Beaton, who sailed across the Northumberland Strait from Prince Edward Island in 1806. Beaton made the journey with his elderly mother, a refugee from the Scottish Highlands, and his brother Alexander. They were searching for somewhere to begin a fresh start in life. As their tiny craft approached the land, the boys hopped out and carried their mother to shore. She looked around at this unfamiliar new land and must have been impressed. "This is the place," she declared in Gaelic. Today you'll find the Beaton name throughout the Mabou area.

The next stretch is all downhill.

11.3   Hang a LEFT at the T.

11.5   The ledge road to the left is actually an old railbed leading to the Mabou coal mines.

The **Mabou coal mines** operated for about five years in the early 1900s. The village that grew around the mines included a store, school and Presbyterian church. About thirty-five families lived in company row houses, similar to the ones in downtown Inverness. Unfortunately, the coal seams ran very close to the ocean floor. Unlike the Sydney Coal Field, whose lateral uniform seams formed in a marine basin, the Mabou field formed inland, in a limnic basin. So its seams are thick and chunky. That makes them tricky to mine underwater. The sea can seep between the seams or through cavities created when miners tunnel through the abrupt end of a seam. The Mabou coal mines closed in 1909 when a tunnel too close to the seabed caved in and flooded. When the mining company shut down the operation the village shut down too. A proposed hotel was never built.

Feel free to bike down the railbed to get to the mines. But don't expect to find a ghost town. The old village is long gone. If you walk the coast you'll find plenty of coal, fossils and petrified wood. Be very careful exploring.

Turn left for the optional side trip. It's 2.9 km return. Otherwise, continue STRAIGHT.

14.1   Pass the wharf road.

15.2   Turn RIGHT onto the MacDonald Glen Road. The road looks like a narrow driveway to a white house with green trim about 150 m away.

16.6   Descend into MacDonald Glen.

> A **glen** is just a narrow valley. You'll find them wedged between the mountains all over Inverness County: MacIsaacs Glen, Pipers Glen, Glendyer, Skye Glen, Glenville, Glen Campbellton, etc., each with its own character and history. The passage through MacDonald Glen follows the old priest route between Broad Cove and the former Catholic church across Mabou Harbour.

Continue following the road down the hill and over the bridge. You can see where it picks a path along the base of the mountains further ahead.

17.4   Keep RIGHT at the V.

17.9   Keep STRAIGHT past a left offshoot.

18.4   For the next 200 m the road and brook tend to change places. Detour the wet stuff by walking your bike through a narrow path to the right of the new stream.

18.6   The road and stream split apart. A tough climb awaits.

19.4   Turn LEFT at the crossroads.
      For a quick exit, continue straight down to Northeast Mabou. Follow the river at the bottom of the hill to Northeast Cove. Then turn left and follow the pavement back to Mabou.

21.2   Continue STRAIGHT past Doyles Road.

If you are willing to explore, try finding remnants of abandoned farms along any of the old roads up here. Look for foundations, rock plies, stone walls, apple trees, and rusted containers.

> The **exodus of farmers** from the Cape began in the 1870s. They were attracted here by the good soil, but soon found that the growing season was much too short. Several farmers found employment in the Inverness coal mines, which opened in 1865. Many others took advantage of the new possibilities of transcontinental rail travel and moved to Oregon and Washington state.

21.3   Continue STRAIGHT past a left offshoot.

22.3   Turn RIGHT onto the Glenora Falls road. It's all downhill from here!

For an optional side trip continue straight. You will exit the forest and enter the **Cape Highlands community pasture** 2.8 km from here. The NS Dept. of Agriculture and Marketing manages the land for local farmers who bring their cattle up here to graze. Several families once lived out on the Cape Highlands but today you'll find only cows. They pretty much mind their own business but several will line up along the roadside fence to watch as you pass. Thirty years ago these stomping grounds were almost exclusively for sheep.

27.3   Turn RIGHT onto Route 19.

27.8   Pass one of the area's last remaining sheep farms on the right.

29.6   Turn RIGHT. This scenic road descends along the back of Mabou Mountain.

31.8   Keep LEFT at the maple syrup sign.

33.3   Keep LEFT at the white house. Cross the bridge and continue following the Northeast Mabou River.

33.8   Turn LEFT at the bridge over Northeast Cove. Follow this paved road back to Mabou Hall. For post-ride eats try the Shining Waters Bakery at the junction of Route 19.

Colindale Road

Starting Point: The Port Hood Courthouse off Route 19 in Inverness County. If court is in session the beach parking lot behind the courthouse may be your best bet.

Distance: 23.8 km
Difficulty: moderate; several small hills
Trail type: mostly gravel road; some pavement
Riding Time: half day or less

The Colindale Road begins in Port Hood and follows the warm waters of the Northumberland Strait. Long before Port Hood became a mining town, its riches lay in the sea. Early visitors to Nova Scotia rarely missed a chance to reap the province's natural treasures, and by the 1700s French and Jersey fishing fleets had discovered cod in St.Georges Bay and the Northumberland Strait. They would arrive early in the summer and stay for the season. When the temperatures dropped, they would retreat to Europe with their catch while the sea turned to ice behind them. It was impossible to fish the Northumberland Strait in winter anyway as it became jammed with drift ice from the Gulf of St. Lawerence.

The town got its name in 1767, in honour of Admiral Hood, the commander in chief of British naval forces in North America. By this time the French had left, as Louisbourg had fallen for good. A new generation of permanent settlers, Loyalists and later the Irish and Scottish, took their place on the land and at sea. The harbour continued to boom for at least another hundred years. In 1880 boats in the harbour were so tightly packed together that people could safely walk across the channel to Port Hood Island by jumping from one shipdeck to the next. Since then, people have worked in the coal mines, the ice processing industry and on their farms. And of course a few still turn to the sea.

Port Hood has produced its share of fine athletes as well. Duncan Gillis brought home a silver medal in the hammer throw from the 1912 Stockholm

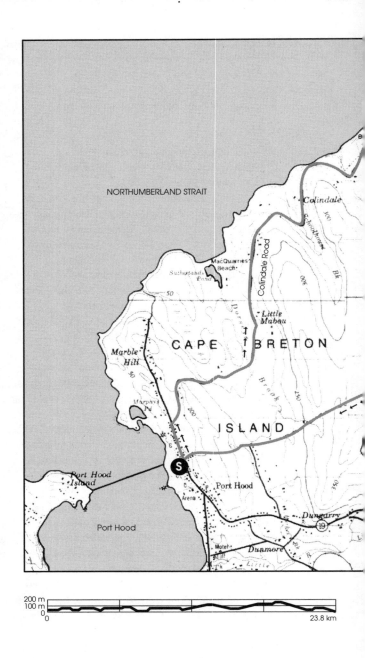

NORTHUMBERLAND STRAIT

Colindale

Collindale Road

MacQuarries Beach

Sutherlands Pond

Little Mabou

C A P E   B R E T O N

Marble Hill

Murphy Pd

I S L A N D

Port Hood Island

S

Port Hood

Arena

Port Hood

Dungarry
19

Motel

Dunmore

200 m
100 m
0
0   23.8 km

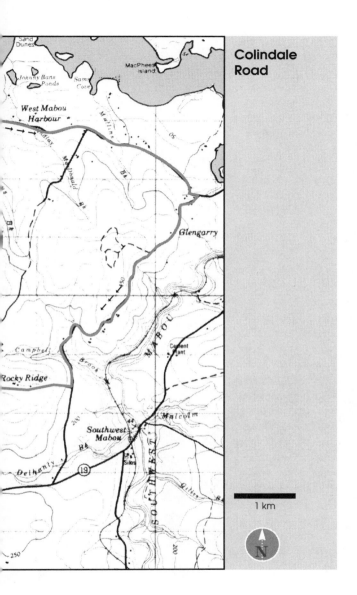

Colindale
Road

1 km

N

Olympics. He also led his teammates into the opening ceremonies as the Canadian flagbearer for those games. Gillis's other achievements include once defeating American great Jim Thorpe and later becoming the Canadian heavyweight wrestling champ. Hockey fans will be more familiar with NHL all-star defenceman Al MacInnis, noted for his rocket from the point.

0.0   Turn LEFT out of the courthouse parking lot. Port Hood Island is on the left along this stretch.

Looking back over Mabou Harbour from Glengarry.

The natives used to call the Port Hood area *kegweomkek*, or "sand bar," in reference to a **land bridge** that once connected the island to the mainland. It's an appropriate name considering how the quest to connect the two land masses has tested the ingenuity and patience of Port Hooders for several decades. The isthmus, which stretched across to Murphys Point, protected the early European fishing ships until a storm broke it apart in 1819. Another breakwater lasted until the 1830s. Many skippers returning from the Strait resented having to tack all the way around to the southern harbour approach, especially when the sea became restless. The north route was more direct so they cut a hole in the barrier. It was just a small opening, but when the sea started nibbling away at its edges there was no turning back. The tide eventually washed away the barrier and any hopes of plugging the hole. Thirty years later the breakwater had completely disappeared.

The line of rocks that cross the harbour today are leftovers from a public works project that began in 1904. The federal government hired people to work on the land bridge every three or four years, often preceding an election. The on again /off again marathon continued into the 1950s. As you can tell, they never quite finished.

You'll also notice several rock escarpments lining the Port Hood Island shoreline. Some of the rock probably went into the breakwater, but most of it had been quarried two hundred years earlier by the French. Most of Fortress Louisbourg and some French forts in the West Indies were constructed with stone taken from Port Hood Island.

0.6   Turn RIGHT onto the Colindale Road.
This road originated as a narrow walking trail between neighbors.

4.9   Finally some scenery!

This coastal farming region was settled by middle-class Scots who came to Cape Breton in droves between 1805 and 1835. Unlike poorer Scottish immigrants who got booted off their land, the **Colindale farmers** came for economic reasons. The end of the clan system in the Scottish highlands and islands meant that men were no longer hired to go off and fight wars away from home. Thus, most stayed put with little to do. Healthier diets and a smallpox vaccine ensured that fewer people were dying. There just was not enough decent land to go around. And so they sailed to Nova Scotia. Many of the original 200 acre land grants on this road are still intact.

5.2   See the Cape Mabou Highlands from the crest of the hill.

5.6   The old Colindale Road School is on the right.

5.8   Cross Schoolhouse Brook. Some of the older folks around here may recall their teacher sending them down to the brook first thing in the morning to fetch the day's drinking water.

7.0   The points that jut into the strait on Cape Mabou ahead are, from nearest to furthest: Green Pt., Beaton Pt., Coal Mine Pt. and Finlay Pt.

10.3   Hit pavement.

10.9   Go STRAIGHT.

11.7   Keep STRAIGHT past the New Ferry Road.

12.1   Pass the resting place of many early settlers.

12.6   Pass the West Mabou Sports Club on the left.

Cape Mabou, as seen from the Colindale Road.

If you and your cycling partner(s) get an itchin' to do some square dancing to traditional Cape Breton fiddle music, then this is the place. Come back on Saturday night, sometime "around tenish." Everyone is welcome and you don't need to know a thing about traditional dance.

12.9 Mabou is across the water under the white church steeple.

13.3 Hang a RIGHT. Sneak a peak over your left shoulder a few times as you head up this hill.

14.3 Catch your breath and take a look around.

Right around here is where **Benjamin Worth**, Gelngarry's first permanent resident, settled down. Worth sailed up here from Princeton, New Jersey, around 1786 to put some distance between himself and a young United States. The Americans busted Worth as a British spy during the American Revolution. They showed their disappointment by branding a "T" (for Tory or traitor) on the man's hand. Perhaps the traitor wasn't too excited about what might happen next when he decided to flee; other Red Coat spies ended up dangling from a noose.

Being first in town, Worth managed to snag the best farmland, a south-facing slope down to the river, protected from the north and west winds.

15.9   The Southwest Mabou River meanders below.

See the highway bridge down there? It was built in 1955 to replace the span that got wrecked during the **Great Southwest Mabou Beer Spill of '53**. A beer truck actually fell through the old rotten bridge while en route to Inverness. No one was hurt. In fact the crash began what turned out to be a very good week for the locals. It transformed the river into the most popular spot in the county. No one guarded the brew so people came from miles around to collect all they could. Some drank the free beer on the river-banks, others carried it home in large sacks. The smart beer collectors hid as much as they could in the woods above the old train tracks (just right of the river). Then they'd sneak back later to collect their loot. There was so much traffic through the woods that new paths emerged between the beer and surrounding villages.

18.1   Take a 90° RIGHT at Earl Doncaster's blue mailbox.

The road looks like a private driveway, but it's actually the old stagecoach route to Port Hood. It will take you back to the courthouse. Surveyed in the 1820s, the road ran from Port Hood, across the Mull River to Whycocomagh. Some sections of the trail are still intact but others, like the piece behind Earl's mailbox down to the river, have grown in completely. Its use dwindled after a rare east wind toppled trees over the road and made several sections impassable.

19.0   Pass through open pastureland and by a white house.

19.8   At the better dirt road keep LEFT.

20.1   Cut RIGHT, up the hill.

20.6   Good view of Port Hood, Port Hood Island, and Henrys Island here. Cape George is across the bay.

22.5   Go RIGHT at the T.
    If staying clean and dry matters to you, go LEFT here and return to Port Hood via Route 19.

22.6   Unless it's been fixed, there's one mighty deep mud pit here.

23.8   When you get back to the courthouse consider cooling off at the beach down the hill. The Northumberland Strait boasts the warmest waters north of the Carolinas! The Nova Scotia Lifeguard Service supervises the beach during the summer until 6:00 P.M.

River Denys Mountain

Starting Point: St. Mary's Parish Catholic Church in Glendale, nearly 25 km northeast of the Canso Causeway on Highway 105.

Length:	18.7 km
Difficulty:	moderate at first, then easy
Trail Type:	poorly maintained gravel on the way up, narrow wagon track on the way back
Riding time:	less than half a day

This tour taps into just one of the nearly infinite mountain biking routes in Inverness County's Creignish Hills and Ainslie Uplands. The Hills run along the north side of Highway 105 between Port Hastings and Whycocomagh, with the Ainslie Uplands tucked behind them. This rugged region, which lies in the triangle bounded by the 105, Lake Ainslie and the sea, is crisscrossed by an extensive (and confusing) labyrinth of old cart tracks, back-country farm roads and new forestry roads. If exploring beyond the River Denys Mountain loop, be sure to bring a compass and a detailed topo map. The forest has reclaimed a few of the old roads that are mapped, while newer roads didn't make the cut for the last map edition. Most roads look the same, several dead end (or never end), and the disoriented cyclist could spend the day(s) pedalling around in circles, miles from the nearest farmhouse or well-travelled highway.

Things would have been much safer if we could warp back a few generations. Back then the (not so) old cart tracks linked bustling farming villages. Wet cow patties might have posed the biggest obstacles. Because people still use several of the cart trails for recreation or accessing woodlots, many of them are still intact. The villages, on the other hand, have almost completely disappeared. These communities started spreading across the landscape in the mid 1800s. In those days a family could still survive on a few acres of land, a good work ethic and a neighbour to barter with. St. Margaret of Scotland Church now stands alone in a young hardwood forest (formerly the village of River Denys Mountain) as a monument to these times. This isolated church is one of the only built attractions on this tour.

0.0   Reset your odometer at the eastern end of the parking lot, near the mailboxes. Turn RIGHT onto Highway 105.

0.1   Continue STRAIGHT past the MacInnis Road. This is where you come back out.

0.5   Keep going STRAIGHT.

0.9   Continue STRAIGHT past the Maple Brook Road.

2.4   Follow the sign to River Denys Mountain. Turn LEFT.

3.1   To the left you can see the sugar maple—yellow birch—beech forest that grows on the Creignish Hills' undisturbed slopes. More hardwoods create a pleasant riding atmosphere heading up alongside McColls Brook.

5.2   Ignore the right offshoot.

5.7   Pass by a few driveways on the left, including one that leads to the Cape Clear Snow-mobilers club house. You've probably noticed some of their signs on the trail.

7.2   Continue STRAIGHT, for now, and merge with the River Denys Road, which enters from the left. You are now in the abandoned village of River Denys Mountain, settled by Catholic Scots around 1840.

7.3   Turn RIGHT and head to the church.

7.4   St. Margaret of Scotland church is all that
remains of the village.

The **St. Margaret of Scotland church,**
built in 1841, was the community's centre for the
thirty to forty families that lived up here well into
the early 1900s. The road you were just on, which
continues north to MacLeod Settlement (current
population: zero) would have been lined by potato
fields, vegetable gardens and pastureland for sheep
and cattle. Ditto for the east/west running River
Denys Road, on which you are now standing. In
addition to allowing the settlers to visit their neighbours, the local blacksmith shop or the CNR trains
down in the valley, these roads served as important
thoroughfares for long distance voyagers. (The River
Denys Road continues west for ten miles to Judique
on St. Georges Bay.) The local history book quotes
some "long dead chauvinist" traveller complaining
that "the longest things in the world are a woman's
tongue, a clergyman's pocket, and the River Denys
Road."

As for the church, the story goes like this:
Once upon a time (in the 1820s), a young woman
from Malagawatch, on Bras d'Or Lake, ran away
from home. Her Presbyterian parents either object-
ed to her plans to marry a Roman Catholic man or
had forbidden her from becoming a nun (the story
has a few variations, depending on who you talk to).
In any event, they weren't getting along so she split.
Apparently the young lass laid down to rest where
the church now stands. During her sleep she dreamt
that someday a church would be built in this spot
and from it would flow beautiful music. We can
only assume that she got to wherever she was headed and lived happily ever after.

River Denys Mountain

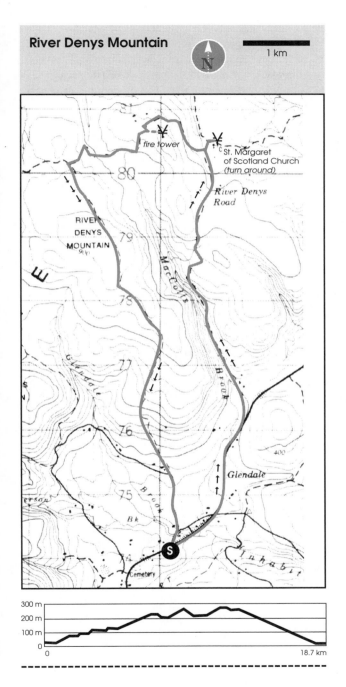

1 km

fire tower

St. Margaret
of Scotland Church
(turn around)

River Denys
Road

RIVER
DENYS
MOUNTAIN

MacTouls

Brook

E

80

79

78

77

76

75

Glendale

B k

Glendale

Brook

400

S

Cemetery

Inhabit

300 m
200 m
100 m
0

0   18.7 km

> Dispossessed Eiggers (Scots from the Isle of Eigg; they got the boot from their homeland when their land barons decided sheep made better tenants) fulfilled the first part of the woman's dream in 1841. The church served Catholics from miles around for about a century. It was such a popular place of worship that in 1889 the village had to split the building in two and stick another piece in the middle. But the church had no organ or other instruments and therefore no music. Now, fifty years after the last farmers had finally left the mountain, the second part of the young lasse's dream comes true each summer. St. Margaret of Scotland gets packed once every July for the **Musique Royale** concert. This travelling ensemble, whose talents include harpsichord and cello, play to a full house whenever they visit River Denys Mountain. For more info, call the municipal office in Port Hood. Besides Musique Royale "unplugged," the church hosts a "ski-doers mass" each winter and one service in the summer.
>
> The pioneer Eiggers rest peacefully in the cemetery behind the wooden crucifix. Their epitaphs are engraved in Gaelic.

To leave, head back the way you came.

7.5   Hang a LEFT and continue retracing your treads.

7.6   Turn RIGHT and head west along the River Denys Road. The local schoolhouse used to be on the southwest corner.

8.9   Go STRAIGHT.

Hang a LEFT for an optional sidetrip to the fire tower. Remember to turn off your odometer if heading left. On a clear day you can gaze across six counties from the top of the tower (all four in Cape Breton plus Antigonish and Guysborough on the mainland).

Over the horizon appears a fishing boat, land locked in someones backyard.

11.5 Hang a LEFT at the T.

Although it starts off looking pretty much like the other rocky 4x4 roads up here, the route to the left quickly becomes inaccessible to vehicles. After about a kilometre the trail narrows as young hardwoods crowd its edges. The trees hang overhead and in many places transform the trail into a dark tunnel.

11.9 Keep LEFT.

14.6 Continue STRAIGHT past the right offshoot and re-enter the tunnel.

14.9 Continue STRAIGHT past a couple offshoots on the left.

15.5 An offshoot to the left here leads to one of the Creignish Hills' abandoned farmhouses. Only a foundation and stone wall remain.

16.4 Avoid the old spikes sticking out of a rotting culvert.

17.1 Pass by a house and large field on the right.

17.4 Turn LEFT at the MacInnis Road.

18.3 Continue STRAIGHT. Then cross a brook.

18.6 A RIGHT here will bring you back to the church where you started.

VICTORIA COUNTY

St. Anns Bay

Starting Point: Two kilometres northeast of the Englishtown ferry off Route 312 in Victoria County. Park on the side of the road where the pavement ends, but not on the clearing where the school bus turns.

Length:	10.5 km return
Difficulty:	difficult but short
Trail Type:	rocky wagon track
Riding Time:	half day or less

     The St. Anns Bay trail, near Englishtown, begins in an area with a rich cultural history. Despite Englishtown's name, the French were here earlier. Back in 1629 a French captain, Charles Daniel, was sailing to Quebec with supplies and men when a fierce storm drove him into the bay. The natives told him not to bother resuming his journey, since Quebec had been taken a month earlier by the English. So Daniel decided to stay put and build a fort at the mouth of St. Anns Harbour. A monument near the Englishtown ferry now marks the spot. The French later established a naval base here. Things quieted down after 1719 when the French government decided Louisbourg would make a better location for a strong fortress and territory capital. While on the trail, keep an eye out for daffodils, the telltale sign of the French presence that has lasted to this day. These flowers are not indigenous to Nova Scotia and historians doubt that the British would have planted them.

     The Brits came in the 1780s, but Englishtown didn't receive its present name until 1820. Scottish settlers referred to the village as *Bhal na Ghul* or "town of the English" because the Brits couldn't speak Gaelic.

     Englishtown is best known, though, for its most famous son, the 7'9"/425 lb giant Angus MacAskill. MacAskill was born in 1825 in the Hebrides off of Scotland and moved with his family to Englishtown at the age of six. He later travelled with P. T. Barnum's circus throughout Europe and America. One of his most famous acts was with the legendary

Tom Thumb. Their act involved a mock fight with Tom
Thumb dancing on the giant's outstretched palm.
(MacAskill's hand was 6 in. wide and twice as long).
Thumb would then jump into MacAskill's pocket. After
his travels with the circus the giant returned home to
Englishtown to manage a small mill and store. Today
MacAskill rests peacefully in his 13 ft. long casket at the
Englishtown Cemetery. For more information on
MacAskill and his hometown, visit the Giant MacAskill
Museum, 3.5 km west of the Englishtown ferry on
Route 312.

      The trail itself follows high above the eastern
shore of St. Anns Bay along the edge of Kluscap (also
known as Kellys) Mountain. It's basically just a couple
of big ups and downs. Toe clips (or clipless pedals) will
help on the ups and, if you've got it, suspension will
smooth out the downs. The days of outdoor adventure
on this mountain may be numbered due to a proposed
quarry. The Department of Natural Resources is ass-
esing whether Kluscap, a sacred place of aboriginal
spirituality, should be given protected status.

0.0   Reset your odometer at the wooden bridge
over Sally's Brook. The bridge is about 250 m
from where the pavement ends.

0.1   Keep RIGHT.

0.5   Pass Oyster Pond on your left.

0.8   Cross over the iron bridge that crosses Mac-
Donald's Brook. This bridge is unmistakable;
it's covered with rust and has no railing.
Prepare for the first of the trail's two mother
hills: a gradual but rocky 122 m climb.

1.6   You've reached the top! Take a breather and
then tackle a rocky downhill section.

2.9   Take the bridge across Smiths Brook. Years of
erosion have exposed the large boulders that

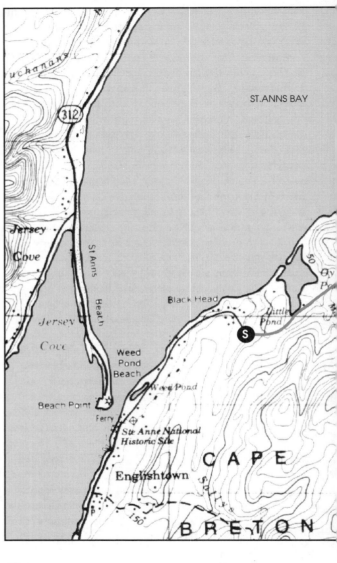

ST. ANNS BAY

Jersey
Cove

St Anns Beach

Jersey
Cove

Black Head

Little
Pond

Weed
Pond
Beach

Weed Pond

Beach Point

Ferry

Ste Anne National
Historic Site

Englishtown

CAPE

BRETON

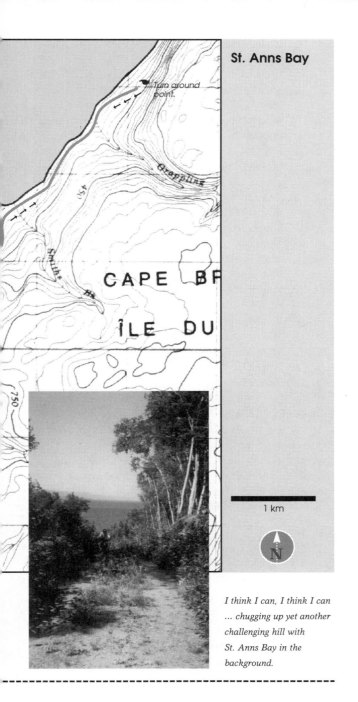

St. Anns Bay

Turn around point.

Grappling

CAPE BR

ÎLE DU

1 km

N

I think I can, I think I can ... chugging up yet another challenging hill with St. Anns Bay in the background.

underlie this landscape. If you're willing to ditch your bike for a few minutes, hop along these boulders down to the water. You'll reach a rocky beach and be rewarded with a fantastic view of St. Anns Bay. Waves have washed large piles of logs and branches up onto the back of the beach, so you may have a little trouble getting out to the shoreline. Another climb awaits upon your return from the beach.

3.2   The hill peaks and you begin another gradual descent. This portion of the trail provides another view of St. Anns Bay.

3.9   Another hill: short and steep.

4.1   Follow the trail along a steep ledge. The road is slowly falling into the bay here and it looks like some of the leaning birches will follow.

These hills were too steep for people to settle, and anyone who tried would have been constantly showered by falling earth and rock. However, talus slopes like this one do support very **diverse populations of rodents and other small mammals**. They thrive along these slopes because the steep grades restrict the movements of larger predators like the weasel. Uncommon Southern Bog Lemmings as well as relict species of Rock Vole and Gaspe Shrew have been identified along the steep slopes above St. Anns Bay. (So if something runs out in front of you don't run the little guy over!) They normally occur in more northerly regions or at higher altitudes.

4.4   Cross the bridge over Grappling Brook. The brook has cut quite a gorge into the side of the mountain. Head carefully down to the shoreline of St. Anns Bay to Little Grappling Beach (or wait until the way back). This is a good spot for a swim on a hot day. Looking across the bay you can see the Cabot Trail hugging the coast en route to northern Cape Breton.

From here it's easy to tell why the beauty of the bay appealed to early voyagers. About a hundred years after most of the French bailed out, another ship that would make its way into the local history books visited these waters. She was called the *Ark*, and like Captain Daniel's ship, sought refuge from stormy seas. The ship, sailed by a **Rev. Norman MacLeod** and his deeply loyal followers, was en route to Ohio from Pictou when it entered the bay. Upon discovering their surroundings, MacLeod decreed that God had sent them here and they would go no further. The dispossessed Calvinist preacher from the Scottish Highlands, would soon become the "prophet, priest, and king" of St. Anns. He ruled with an iron fist and according to strict religious doctrines. Some people figured he was completely nuts, but most took his word as law.

As an example of MacLeod's madness, he once rounded up everyone's skates after two boys had fallen through the ice one Sunday and drowned. He would not tolerate these "evil devices of Sabbath desecration" in his village. So the preacher cut a hole in the ice and consigned the blades to the bottom of the sea. The same thing happened to all the ladies' crimping irons when MacLeod found out they were using them to enhance their appearance.

The story ends in the 1850s. After a disastrous potato harvest in 1848, the "Normanites" decided to try their luck in Australia. MacLeod's son lived down under and figured the Englishtown people would find life much easier there. Between 1851 and 1858 six ships carrying at least 883 people sailed out of this bay for a twenty-week voyage to the other side of the world. Australia turned out to be a bust, but the weary travellers finally found happiness in New Zealand.

The bridge over Smiths Brook, just upstream from St. Anns Bay.

4.6   You may begin to notice more and more larger softwoods.

> **Giant hemlocks and spruce** were part of the bay's lure to early visitors. The French, Brits, Normanites and their descendants who stuck around have been felling them for generations. Big ships and houses have always required a lot of good timber. As you get further away from the flatter populated areas these trees are more prevalent.
>
> Old eastern hemlocks and red spruce so close to the abundant marine life in St. Anns Bay is a welcome combination for the bald eagle. The birds build their large nests on the flat tops of these old trees. And thanks to a sprinkling of older deciduous trees, there are plenty of woodpeckers around here too (you can hear them: they go "peck, peck, peck," but really fast!).

5.2   The road seems to stop here for no particular reason. Have a snack by the giant hemlock and head back to Englishtown.

Our thanks to Tom Wilson for suggesting this trail.

Boularderie and the Bras d'Or

Starting Point: The junction of the Matheson Road and the Kempt Head Road in Victoria County. Take Exit 13 off Highway 105 and go 4.5 km southwest of Ross Ferry.

Length: 13.7 km
Difficulty: easy
Trail Type: maintained dirt road
Riding Time: less than half a day

This loop around the tip of Boularderie Island offers an easy ride along a quiet backcountry road that follows the shore of Great Bras d'Or Lake. Its gentle slopes and well-maintained surface make this an attractive route for a leisurely or family outing (for more challenging terrain take Highway 105 to the St. Anns Bay trail in Englishtown). The road follows the shoreline down the Bras d'Or Channel and back along St. Andrew's Channel, exposing the cyclist to panoramic views of the lake and surrounding hills.

Boularderie Island was first settled by the French and later by Scots. The early settlers, who came with the son of French naval officer M. Poupet de la Boularderie around 1740, found the land to be quite fertile. Generations of island folk have been working the land ever since, combining subsistence agriculture with small-scale woodcutting. Although farming is still the mainstay of Boularderie Island, many of the small family farms that used to line the Kempt Head Road have long been abandoned. People still cut small quantities of wood here, and the resulting patchwork of regenerating fields and woodlots at varying successional stages provides habitat for a wide diversity of bird species. Bird-watchers can bring binoculars on this smooth road without having to worry about them getting tossed around as they ride.

On our way to the Matheson Road (where the ride starts), we'll pass through the community of Ross Ferry. This place hasn't seen much action since 5:00 P.M. on November 8, 1961. That's when the Seal Island

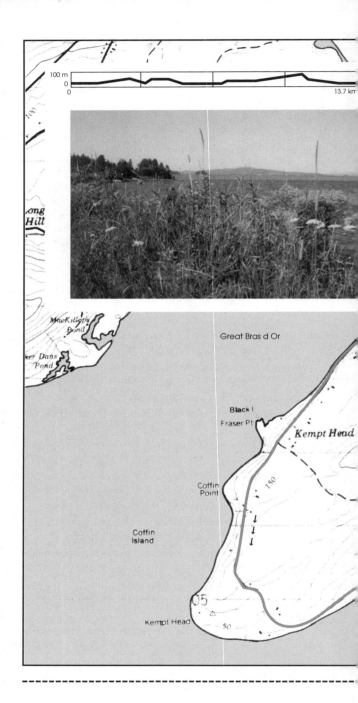

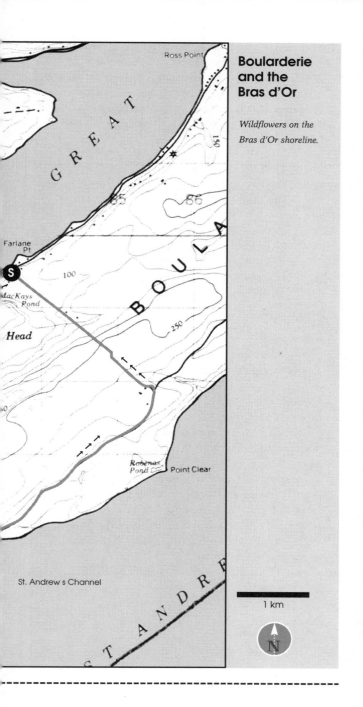

Boularderie
and the
Bras d'Or

Wildflowers on the
Bras d'Or shoreline.

Ross Point

GREAT

BOULA

Farlane
Pt

MacKays
Pond

Head

Robenas
Pond

Point Clear

St. Andrew s Channel

1 km

N

Bridge at the bottom of Kellys Mountain opened. Before the bridge's construction, ferries shuttled 180,000 cars per year between the Ross Ferry dock and Big Harbour. Most of the ferries over the years were hand-me-downs form the Canso Strait crossing. In the days before automobiles, a Captain Matheson and his wife ran a scow for travellers and their horses.

0.0 Begin where the road from Ross Ferry meets the Matheson Road.

0.3 Pass over a small bridge.
MacKays Pond is to the left. The Bras d'Or Channel is on your right. Looking southwest across the water you can see the opening of St. Patrick's Channel. The channel extends nearly 50 km to Whycocomagh.

The **Bras d'Or** (meaning "arm of gold") **Lakes** formed at the close of the last ice age after melting glaciers flooded a deep valley. This inland sea supports a unique marine ecosystem characterized by a very deep bottom, low salinity and negligible tidal action. Consequently, it supports a diverse collection of both fresh- and saltwater aquatic life. Creatures that call the Bras d'Or home range from oysters and harbour seals to rainbow trout. The sheltered waters of the Bras d'Or are also calm and free of fog, making them a world-renowned yachting destination. The Bras d'Or Yacht Club in Baddeck has held a regatta on the lake every year since 1904.

Rising out of the lake at two o'clock is Beinn Bhreagh (pronounced "beyn bree-ya," Gaelic for "beautiful mountain").

The inventor **Alexander Graham Bell** climbed Beinn Bhreagh with his family in 1886, ten years after inventing the telephone. It was from this summit, where Bell could reach out and touch the beautiful Bras d'Or, that he found his greatest calling. Charmed by the tranquillity of the landscape below, Bell set about purchasing farms on the headland. Seven years later he owned the entire mountain. During his summers at Beinn Bhreagh, Bell carried out many of the experiments that contributed to his important discoveries in the fields of aviation, medicine, marine engineering and teaching the deaf. Bell's experiments included breeding multi-nippled sheep and angora goats, developing a simple machine to distil drinking water from Bras d'Or seawater, flying tetrahedral kites, and testing early flying machines and hydrofoils. The 1909 flight of the *Silver Dart* over Baddeck Bay, just behind Beinn Bhreagh, was the first heavier-than-air flight in the British Empire. Bell and Frederick Baldwin, a partner in the *Silver Dart* project, also used the waters around Beinn Bhreagh to test hydrofoils. In 1919, their fourth prototype hydrodrome, HD-4, became the world's fastest boat when it skimmed over the bay at 114 km/h. Bell, who died in 1922, is buried at Beinn Bhreagh along with his wife. The Alexander Graham Bell National Historic Site in Baddeck is open daily between 9:00 A.M. and 9:00 P.M. (It closes at 5:00 P.M. between October 1 and June 30).

The white cliffs directly across the Bras d'Or Channel expose the **gypsum** that underlies much of this part of Cape Breton. The gypsum comes from deposits laid down some 360 million years ago when a large marine basin covered this region. Several spots along the lake have been mined for gypsum over the past two hundred years. Besides sailboats, traffic in the channel today consists largely of ocean-going vessels from Little Narrows (about 30 km down St. Patrick's Channel) that rely on this waterway to export gypsum to cities in the United States. The passage between Boularderie Island and the gypsum cliffs is the only natural channel through which seafaring ships can access ports on the Bras d'Or.

To the southwest (about one o'clock) you should see **Spectacle Island Game Sanctuary**. That's the tiny island near the southern edge of St. Patrick's Channel. Spectacle Island is an important breeding site for the **double-breasted cormorant.** These shorebirds usually nest on sea cliffs or in trees along the coast, but on islands such as this, their droppings often kill all of the trees. In such instances they will breed on the ground and make their nests with, among other things, seaweed. The cormorant's appetite for fish has long made them a target for people who worried that they were depleting fish stocks. However, most studies done on the cormorant indicate that they do not go after the same species that we value.

2.2   Continue STRAIGHT past the private road on your left.

3.8   Pass by the old field at Coffin Point on your right.

4.2   Proceed up the day's first hill. Both sides of the hill are bordered by mature birches. Near the top, especially on the right, you can find samples of several of the hardwood tree species native to the Bras d'Or shoreline: red maples, beeches, yellow birches, white birches, and sugar maples.

5.0   The road swings left and descends towards the other side of Boularderie Island.

> From here, you get an excellent view of the Boisdale Hills. These hills provide some of the finest **bald eagle** breeding habitat in all of eastern North America. Eagles build their nests on large trees close to waters that have an abundant supply of fish. The lowland hills surrounding the Bras d'Or Lake fulfil both of these requirements.
>
> To the right, way off in the distance, the Barra Strait connects the two Bras d'Or lakes. Three hundred immigrants from Barra, Scotland, settled on its shores in 1817.

5.8   Continue past a farm on your left.

6.0   The road becomes narrower and the surrounding forest is now dominated by older softwoods that have grown up on previously cleared land.

8.1   This is probably the most scenic part of the ride. The road skirts the shoreline along the hillside about 4 m above the water. On sunny days, you can feel the warm sunshine squeezing through the trees, interrupted only by the cool breeze off of St. Andrew's Channel. You can score a good view of the channel wherever the trees thin out. St. Andrew's Channel includes the deepest section of the Bras d'Or lakes, with depths measuring up to 275 m.

8.6　　Continue STRAIGHT.

10.5　　Continue STRAIGHT past the offshoot on the right. It's a private road that leads to Point Clear.

11.2　　Turn LEFT onto Matheson Road to head back across the island.

12.2　　You've reached the highest elevation on this route, a modest 80 m above sea level (Parts of St. Andrew's Channel are over three times as deep!). This high point provides a good view across the Bras d'Or Channel to MacDonald Point. You might also want to take a last look for a circling bald eagle overhead.

13.3　　Pavement begins. Coast down the hill to finish the ride.

13.7　　Rendezvous with the road to Ross Ferry.

Our thanks to Tom Wilson for suggesting this loop.

Money Point

Starting Point: The government wharf in Bay St. Lawrence, Victoria County. Turn off the Cabot Trail in Cape North and head north about 15 km. The wharf, the first of two in Bay St. Lawrence, is about 500 m past St. Andrew's Church.

Length:	25.1 km
Difficulty:	killer
Trail Type:	gravel road and rocky wagon track; some pavement
Riding Time:	full day

Is there money at Money Point? We're not sure. Sometime in the 1700s a French payroll ship loaded with gold coins slammed into this rugged promontory of the north Cape Breton coast. She was headed for Louisbourg but lost her valuable cargo on what would later become known as Money Point. For years after the disaster local fishermen sailed or rowed to the crash site with home-made pine-tar mops to scoop up the loot. We don't know much about treasure hunting, but it seems unlikely that these guys would have snagged it all. Unconfirmed reports claim that people have since found coins buried in the surrounding sand or wedged between rocks. The lure of lost riches can appeal to the amateur treasure hunter in all of us at Money Point.

Coins or no coins, the value of this bike trip lies in its rugged terrain and spectacular coastal scenery. And if being isolated from the civilized world adds to your ultimate trail experience, then even better. Money Point is separated from Bay St. Lawrence (both the village and the bay) by a 430 m mountain that juts sharply out of the Cabot Strait.

No one knows this isolation better than Melvin Burton. Melvin, who just opened Burton's Sunset Oasis motel at the base of the mountain in Bay St. Lawrence (phone (902) 383-2666 for reservations), grew up on Money Point. His dad, William, was the lighthouse keeper. The younger Burton recalls a year or

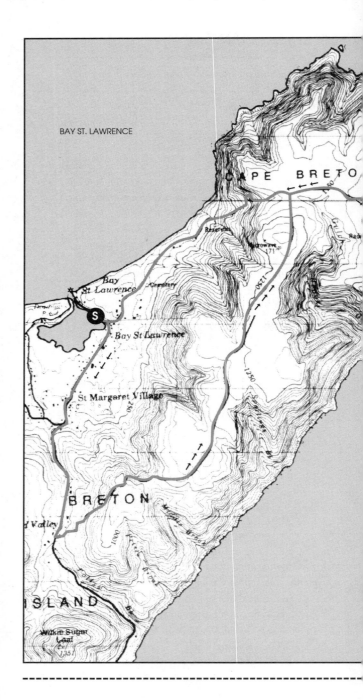

BAY ST. LAWRENCE

Money Point

1 km

From 300 m up, this rocky stretch of the Money Point Road offers a spectacular view of Bay St. Lawrence.

Money Point

SPY BAY

more would sometimes pass between his departures from Money Point. On at least one of these rare trips away from home the little tyke snowshoed across the mountain to visit his grandmother's house on Christmas Eve. There really wasn't much reason to leave. Every August his father would go through the catalogues and order the family a year's worth of supplies and groceries. A ship dropped it all off in September. And once a month or so someone would hike over the mountain to fetch the mail. Melvin had plenty of time to learn his father's profession and at age fourteen the Coast Guard hired him too. For several years the Burtons, either William, Melvin or Melvin's brother Cyril, kept passing ships at a safe distance from the rocky shore with their glowing beacon on Money Point. Since the Coast Guard installed a new automated light in the late 1980s the point has been deserted.

Cycling to Money Point (and getting back) is not easy! It involves a lot of serious climbing and some tricky descents. With the obvious exception of the "rock hop dogs," most of us will have to make the occasional quick dismount to avoid going ass-over-kettle on the descents and landing with a painful groinplant. Unless you're an expert climber expect to do some walking *up* too.

Pack a couple extra PowerBars for this ride and bring plenty of water.

0.0   Turn RIGHT out of the wharf area and head south.

0.2   Continue STRAIGHT. This road is where you return at the end of the day.

1.9   Continue STRAIGHT past the road to Meat Cove.

This road is well worth exploring, either by bike or car. It's a bit like a journey into the Twilight Zone, as **Meat Cove** (bordering on the Pollett Cove-Aspy Fault wilderness), is arguably the most remote community in the Maritimes. The good ol' boys like it that way too. They have been known to run unpopular visitors out of town. You can camp on a cliff at the end of the road for twelve bucks. We recommend the trip.

Some people believe that passing seamen gave Meat Cove its name in 1788. American hunters had illegally slaughtered thousands of moose in the Cape North region the previous winter. The mariners were taken aback by the foul stench of rotting carcasses as their ships passed the cove. Another explanation involves natives chasing Caribou herds over the cliffs and scurrying down to the cove the collect the meat. Caribou haven't roamed Cape Breton since 1912.

3.9   Turn LEFT up a gravel road. There are a couple of garages on the corner at the turn-off.

5.6   The gate and tower on the right mark the end of the day's first brutal climb. This 305 m ascent is good practice for the *real* climb at Money Point.

5.8   The road cuts sharply to the right here. Look to the left for a terrific vista over St. Margaret Village and Deadmans Pool. Another wicked view awaits near the end of the curve, ahead to the right. From up there you overlook Aspy Bay, where half a millennium ago the British conquest of the New World began.

Early in the morning of June 24, 1497, **John Cabot's** ship *Matthew* landed on the mysterious shores of Aspy Bay. After bobbing around for fifty-three days on uncharted waters and unsure of their destination, Cabot and his crew of eighteen had finally found the North American mainland (having previously landed in Newfoundland). The captain and his son Sebastian waded ashore and claimed the new land for King Henry VII. With little fanfare, they erected a cross on the beach and raised the flag of St. George. The rest is history.

While most of us would get pretty excited to find a new continent, Cabot and his crew were actually hoping to drop anchor somewhere around China. By keeping well north of Columbus's route of five years earlier, Cabot figured he might find the mythical western passage to the Orient. Nonetheless, King Henry told Cabot to claim any land he found on his travels just in case. For his efforts, the king gave the explorer £10.

In 1858 Aspy Bay became the terminus of the first cross-Atlantic telegraph cable.

5.9 Expect more views of the countryside below from the clearing on the left. This may be a good spot for a breather before launching an assault up the next hill. Look to the right near the top of this climb for more great views of the bay. North and South Harbour, Dingwall and White Point are all visible.

6.5 The hill levels out and stays relatively flat for another 5 km.

10.0 You can see St. Pauls Island, the "graveyard of the gulf," 24 km offshore.

10.6 Keep STRAIGHT when you pass a road to the towers on the left.

10.9   Keep STRAIGHT. The road to the left is a
           dead end leading to a Coast Guard station.

11.6   Go RIGHT at the T. This is the only road con-
           necting Money Point to Bay St. Lawrence.

A word of caution: If there's only a few hours left
before dusk you'd be smart to bail out now (turn left).
Plan on at least a three-hour journey before you return
to this point. From here to the new lighthouse is about
an hour (or a fraction thereof if you have a deathwish)
and you may need at least two hours of daylight to
guide you back over the mountain. Don't underestimate
the duration of the return trip and remember that
darkness falls quickly on the east side of the mountain.
The road becomes much too steep for anyone to pick
you up, so if you get stuck on Money Point you are on
your own. Ditto for the fool who gets caught there in a
storm. Dark clouds overhead are your cue to turn left.

13.1   The road to the coast cuts down to the LEFT.

           For a worthwhile sidetrip, continue up to the
right. After 600 m you will hit a clearing, the former
site of a microwave tower. At the far end of the clearing a few short walking paths lead to magnificent cliffs
towering 430 m above the deep blue sea. From your
perch you'll probably see plenty of sea birds, ranging
from eagles to guillemonts. Pods of humpback, pilot
and minke whales are also commonly spotted off this
high shore. You may even stumble upon the
Marlborough man suckin' back on a smoke. Even if
you're alone, there are few better places to kick back
and do nothing.
           Remember to take this sidetrip into
account on your odometer readings. (We didn't include
it in our distances.)

13.4   Prepare for the plunge down to the ocean. A
           small clearing, trampled down by countless
           three-point turns, marks the point of no return
           for cars and trucks. This is where it suddenly

dawns on drivers that if they keep going they ain't never coming back. At least not with their vehicle. For cyclists, this hill is something like a downhill ski run: some will torpedo down the trail in a just a few minutes, while it could take those of the chicken-out persuasion nearly an hour to complete the descent. Check your brakes and off you go.

14.8 Pry your fingers off the handlebars, spray some water on those smokin' brake pads, and turn LEFT.

14.9 In a heap of rubble to the right lie the remains of the old Money Point lighthouse.

> The **Money Point light** has been rebuilt in a museum in Ottawa. It floated on a mercury base and received its glow from kerosene. Like an old clock tower, the pull of a dangling 250 lb. weight kept the light rotating. And like clockwork, our lighthouse keeper Melvin cranked that weight every three hours throughout the lonely night. It's fitting, therefore, that Melvin would be the last person to change the bulb before he bid adieu to Money Point in 1976.

16.0 Pass the old wharf. It's been pounded to smithereens by a relentless sea.

16.2 Welcome to Money Point! Stop somewhere below the new light.

There are still a few crumbling foundations here, including the old Burton house. The Coast Guard burnt it down a few years ago. Only Melvin's bathtub and oil tank survived.

The day to day life at **Money Point** was usually uneventful. But when things happened, they happened in a big way. The most exciting day was when the *Carita* made a surprise visit during a snowstorm in January of 1976. She was a 280 ft. bulk storage carrier loaded with crushed peas and oats. According to Melvin, the vessel became disabled off the Magdalen Islands by a fire that took out her radar. The captain of a nearby Norwegian container ship had the *Carita* on his screen and radioed directions to his stranded comrade. But his readings were way off. Without warning the *Carita* slammed into the jagged rocks. Melvin and his brother watched as the crew scurried about her deck like ants. The brothers radioed for help. The Newfoundland ferry was the closest ship to receive the may-day call. They picked up the twenty-eight crew members and ferried them to land, no charge.

A few days later, while the Burton brothers were guarding the scuttled ship against vegetable looters, it split in two. Melvin still vividly remembers that thunderous sound of screeching steel ripping apart. For several months afterwards parts of the shoreline were covered with crushed peas and oats up to the waist. Apparently, it started to really reek in the summer. "The crows wouldn't even touch that crap," Melvin told us.

To the northeast you will see **St. Paul Island**, only eighty nautical miles off Newfoundland's Cape Ray. This desolate rock also has a colourful, albeit more tragic, history of shipwrecks. By the time the British government finally built a couple lighthouses on the island in 1837, it had already claimed several hundred lives. The *Royal Sovereign* slammed into the rock while carrying troops back to England from the War of 1812 battlefield. Only a dozen survived. Three hundred perished when the emigrant ship *Irishman* ran aground. In 1835 St. Paul once claimed four vessels in one night. The list goes on and on....

The cruel irony of St. Paul back then was that even if you were fortunate enough to survive a shipwreck and climb safely onto land, you were still screwed. No one lived on the island, it was a rock; there was nothing to eat, and certainly no radios lying around. Since every self-respecting skipper kept their distance from the unforgiving rock, waving and screaming were completely useless. Survivors would die a slow death as the days turned into weeks.

This horrific scenario is exactly what happened to the poor souls on the *Jessie* around 1825. Some passengers and twenty-six crew members survived the crash. A diary of one of the passengers indicated that the group starved to death over a ten-week period. They had collected driftwood and lit huge bonfires at night in a futile attempt to attract attention.

Every spring, sealers from the mainland and the Magdalen Islands went to St. Paul to find the wrecks from the previous winter. They quietly pocketed any money and valuables, including clothing, that they found on the decomposing corpses.

When you're ready, turn around to leave Money Point.

17.5   Turn RIGHT here for "you know what." It's 370 m of death squeezed into less than a mile. Enjoy! There's a prize for anyone who can get to the top without stopping.

To see the ***Kismet II* shipwreck** keep left for about 300 m. It ran aground during a snowstorm in 1955. Look for old vehicles along this stretch to the left. They are the victims of overconfident drivers, sentenced by a merciless hill to rust here in car purgatory.

19.0   The top. 'Nuff said.

19.3   Keep RIGHT and continue back over the mountain.

20.8   Continue STRAIGHT past the Coast Guard Road.

21.2   Check out the great view of Deadmans Pool and Bay St. Lawrence.

21.4   Look out for rocks! This is where the steep part begins.

22.5   The road improves. The next few hundred metres offer good views of the bay, Black Point and Cape St. Lawrence.

24.2   Pavement begins.

24.4   Pop into Burton's General Store for a well-deserved post-ride snack. You might run into Melvin.

24.9   Go RIGHT and you are finished.

Bicycle Shops & Repair

Andy's Bicycle Repair: 663 Main St., Kingston.
(902) 765-4347

Bicycles Plus: 950 Bedofrd Highway, Bedford.
(902) 832-1700

Hartley Weatherby: 590 Prince Street, Truro.
(902) 893 2087

Cycledelics: 1678 Barrington St., Halifax.
(902) 425-RIDE

Cyclepath: 5240 Blowers St., Halifax. (902) 423-0473

Cyclesmith: 5240 Quinpool Rd., Halifax.
(902) 425-1756 or 492-4236

Dave's Bicycle & Sport Shop: 3523 Plummer Ave.,
New Waterford. (902) 862-8344

Framebreak Bicycle Shop: 102 Webster St., Kentville.
(902) 679-0611

Goodwin's Bike Shop: Rte. 3 Lower Argyle
(Yarmouth Co.). (902) 643-2279

Gord's Sport Centre: 44 Reeves St., Sydney.
(902) 539-4673

Jack Nauss Bicycle Shop: 2571 Robie St., Halifax.
(902) 429-0024

Lunenburg Bicycle Barn: Blue Rocks Rd.,
Lunenburg. (902) 634-3426

Manser's Bicycle Repair: 165 Pleasant St., Yarmouth.
(902) 742-0494

Peak Performance Bicycle Shop: 286 Hawthorne St.,
Antigonish. (902) 863-6722

Phil's Bicycle Shop: downtown Digby. (902) 245-4564.

Ramsay's Cycle and Sport: 229 Kings Rd., Sydney.
(902) 539-1730/7644

Ron's Bicycle Shop: 124 Main St., Dartmouth.
(902)435-0513

Ron's Cycle Shop: Hammond St., Shelburne.
(902) 875-3402

Sportwheels: 209 Sackville Dr., Sackville.
(902) 865-9033/2333

The Trail Shop: 6210 Quinpool Rd., Halifax.
(902) 423-8736

Valley Stove and Cycle: 234 Main St. Wolfville.
(902) 542-7280

Zack's Repair: 10 Pond Rd. North Sydney.
(902) 736-6220

Bicycle Rentals

Adventurequest: Elmsdale. (902) 883-1974.
Crescent Beach Centre: Lockeport. (902) 656-3123.
Cycledelics: 1678 Barrington St., Halifax.
(902) 425-RIDE
Framebreak Bicycle Shop: 102 Webster St., Kentville.
(902) 679-0611
Freewheeling Adventures: RR#1 Hubbards.
(902) 857-3600
Goodwin's Bike Shop: Rte. 3 Lower Argyle
(Yarmouth Co.). (902) 643-2279
Kayak Cape Breton: RR#2 West Bay. (902) 535-3060.
Island Eco-Adventures: Baddeck. (902) 295-3303
Margaree Valley Bike Rentals: Normaway Inn,
Margaree Valley. (902) 248-2987/1-800-565-9463
Island Eco-Adventures: Baddeck. (902) 295-3303
Open Horizons Cycling: Auberge Gisele Country Inn,
Baddeck. (902) 295-2849
Peak Performance Bicycle Shop: 286 Hawthorne St.,
Antoigonish. (902) 863-6722
Pedal & Sea: Halifax International Hostel, 1253
Barrington St., Halifax. (902) 422-3863
Sea Spray Cycle Center: Smelt Brook (near CBH
National Park). (902) 383-2732
The Trail Shop: 6210 Quinpool Rd., Halifax.
(902) 423-8736
Valley Stove and Cycle: 234 Main St., Wolfville.
(902) 542-7280
Wheel Adventures: Tatamagouche. (902) 899-6382

For more information on cycling in the province, contact
Bicycle Nova Scotia
PO Box 3010 South
Halifax, NS B3J 3G6
(902) 425-5450, ext. 316

Selected Bibliography

Bird, W. 1956. *Off-trail in Nova Scotia.* Toronto: Ryerson.

———. 1950. *This is Nova Scotia.* Toronto: Ryerson.

Blomidon Naturalists Society. 1992. *A Natural History of Kings County.* Wolfville: Acadia University.

Cape Breton's Magazine. Various articles.

Creighton, S. F. 1979. *Colchester County: A Pictorial History.* Oxford, Nova Scotia: Municipality of Colchester.

Dennis, C. 1942. *Cape Breton Over.* Toronto: Ryerson.

———. 1937. *More About Nova Scotia.* Toronto: Ryerson.

———. 1934. *Down in Nova Scotia.* Toronto: Ryerson.

Erskine, A. 1992. *Atlas of the Breeding Birds of the Maritime Provinces.* Halifax: Nimbus/NS Museum.

Hamilton, W. 1981. *The Nova Scotia Traveler.* Toronto; Macmillan.

Hall, E. F. (ed). 1981. *Heritage Remembered: The Story of Bear River.* Bear River New Horizons Centre.

Hart, H. C. 1975. *History of the County of Guysborough.* Belleville, Ontario: Mika.

Legends of Inverness County, vol. 1. n.d. Inverness: The Oran.

MacDonald, B. 1973. *The Guysborough Railway 1879-1939.* Halifax: Formac.

MacDonald, N. 1979. *The Broken Ground: A History of Inverness Town.*

Saunders, G. 1970. *Trees of Nova Scotia.* Halifax: Nova Scotia Department of Lands & Forests.

Simmons, M., D. Davis, L. Griffiths, and A. Meuke. 1984. *Natural History of Nova Scotia.* Halifax: Nova Scotia Department of Education and Department of Lands & Forests.

Stevens, D. 1979. *Story of the Musquodoboit Railway.* Musquodoboit Harbour: Yagar Publications.